# Top-Down Confusion

## *Is Gray the New Pink in Education?*

Felecia Nace

ROWMAN & LITTLEFIELD
Lanham • Boulder • New York • London

Published by Rowman & Littlefield
An imprint of The Rowman & Littlefield Publishing Group, Inc.
4501 Forbes Boulevard, Suite 200, Lanham, Maryland 20706
www.rowman.com

Unit A, Whitacre Mews, 26-34 Stannary Street, London SE11 4AB

British Library Cataloguing in Publication Information Available

**Library of Congress Cataloging-in-Publication Data**

Names: Nace, Felecia, author.
Title: Top-down confusion : is gray the new pink in education? / Felecia Nace.
Description: Lanham, MD : Rowman & Littlefield, [2018] | Includes index.
Identifiers: LCCN 2018009453 (print) | LCCN 2018018765 (ebook) | ISBN 9781475831962 (Electronic) | ISBN 9781475831948 (cloth : alk. paper)
Subjects: LCSH: Education--Social aspects--United States. | Educational change--United States. | Education--Philosophy.
Classification: LCC LC191.4 (ebook) | LCC LC191.4 .N33 2018 (print) | DDC 306.430973--dc23
LC record available at https://lccn.loc.gov/2018009453

Printed in the United States of America

# Contents

# Foreword

Everyone is an expert on what's wrong with education today, and few of those people ever get it right. Dr. Nace has done us all a favor by using her knowledge and experience from the front lines in the classroom to the levels of the New Jersey State Department of Education to remind us of some essential truths.

School is supposed to be a place of clarity for the developing child. It is a place of learning and nurturing, where society passes on the wisdom of generations to create functioning adults and citizens. However, schools have become a battleground where politicians posture to show how they're going to improve it, where agenda-ridden interest groups promote their political and social goals, and where "education" corporations ply their wares to make a profit.

What Dr. Nace reminds us is that the one factor being swept up in this nonsense is the child, and she addresses some key hot-button issues, such as religion and gender identity, as well as the very nature of educational leadership and training. She will no doubt anger some people, as perhaps both sides of the argument will claim she's taking sides. She is, but not their respective sides. She's taking the side of the child. She also helps answer the question, "What's a parent to do?"

It is appropriate that she uses the colors gray and pink. "In the pink" can be found in *Romeo and Juliet*, as Mercutio claims, "Why, I am the very pinke of curtesie." Do we have a system that is the very pink of education? No. Things have become muddled and, indeed, gray. There is no "big picture" of what the education system should be doing to be in the pink, except for vague phrases like "let's get back to the 3 Rs," or "more accountability," or "we need to test progress," and countless others.

Most of our lawmakers at the state and national levels are lawyers or businessmen, and by no small coincidence, many of the appointed educational leaders are, as well. Educators don't pretend to be experts on the law or running a business, yet the legislators have no such compunctions. They are swamping educators—teachers and administrators—with paperwork and testing in the name of accountability.

The state, for example, insists on testing special education kids, kids with all sorts of learning and coping issues, at the elementary-school level so they can get an accurate "data picture of progress," without regard for the impact on the child who has to sit in front of the computer and get increasingly frustrated. What are they really accomplishing? They are enriching test manufacturers and packaged learning companies. You can't apply a business model to education. Stop trying! Children are not widgets. It is good that she points this out. Some of the stories she relates are downright horrifying.

The "big picture" we need is offered by Dr. Nace: systems thinking. Let's look at the interplay of child, parent, teacher, administrator, school board, and state department of education, and realize that unless you get these component parts working together as a smooth-running engine, you will not benefit the child. Each has an equally important role to play. One factor should not be imposing on another factor or factors. She uses systems analysis as a model for how we should look at the interaction of these factors.

While you hear the phrase "higher-order thinking skills" spouted at a mind-numbing rate, Dr. Nace suggests ways to approach many of the higher-order thinking skills to be used to address controversial issues. Rather than just take positions, let's learn how to think, maybe even together. Unless there is cooperation and respect among these groups, you will not have progress. Worst of all, this lack of harmony negatively impacts the very children we are supposed to be helping.

No single group has the moral high ground here. Each can and do positively contribute, but they also often operate against the others. For example, state departments of education try to turn their teachers into robotic "facilitators" with no permission to innovate. Superintendents and principals want to be bosses rather than educational leaders. Poorly trained teachers become "yeoman" educators, dutifully trudging chapter by chapter through their texts and assigned curriculum with the awareness that innovation attempts by a creative teacher could be viewed as insubordination.

Parents use the opportunity when their child has a problem to go rushing in on their white charger to show their kids how much they love them. Various interest groups are more interested in promoting their cause than considering the impact on the child. We've lost our way, possibly because our society is not the homogeneous community it once was or because our society has become more impersonal or because both parents have to work and have less time for their child. You can pick your reasons.

Dr. Nace addresses these issues and offers thoughtful insights for parents, teachers, administrators, and lawmakers. I spent forty years in education, and my experience tells me it would be good for all of us to pay attention.

—Peter J. Tamburro Jr.

# Acknowledgments

To God be the glory for the completion of this work.

This book is dedicated to my parents, Ronnie and Opal. Thank you for the gift that keeps giving—a solid foundation in my early years!

To my maternal grandmother, Levada, bravo for being the first in our family to attend college, and the first school teacher in our family as well. You are an inspiration!

To my paternal grandmother, Katherine, thank you for all of the spiritual lessons. I hold them dear to my heart!

The readers of my work sometimes agreed to disagree, which I welcomed. To my steadfast readers—Lawrence Bahnamen, Ken Chwatek, Ty Moore, Ralph Italo Schmidt, Pete Tamburro, Wendy Weinstein, and Pastor Tim Wolfe—I could not have produced this book without your time, attention to detail, and meaningful feedback. Each one of you approached the task as if this were your own work, and I am forever indebted.

A special thank you to my young readers, who provided me with unique insights: Taylor Hickey and Isia Wright.

# Chapter One

# The Graying of Teaching and Learning

Truth is so rare that it is delightful to tell it. —Emily Dickinson

Long gone are the days of black and white in education. Theories and theorists abound in school systems today, so much so that lines regarding how to teach and what to teach consistently get blurred. When mixing the colors black and white, one will end up with the color gray. Since very little in education is clear-cut anymore, largely due to politics and money at play, parents and educators remain in a constant state of uncertainty. That perplexed state is known as a *gray zone.*

However, there was a long period of time in America and other cultures in which education was uncomplicated. Teachers clearly had a voice when changes were needed, and how those changes would take shape. Educators were well respected in the community. Parents understood their second grader's math homework.

Kids played outside without any technological tools—imagine that! This period was known as "being in the pink." As educating children began to be viewed as a more complex process, there was a general feeling that social improvements and academic strides were being made in schools. However, complexity does not always equate with progress. Still, with all of the changes that schools are enduring, many parents and educators are dissatisfied with the path of education. So, just what are the gray areas in teaching and learning?

Currently, there are five major gray areas in education that have captured media attention in the United States, and which require collaboration of all

shareholders to bring clarity to what has become obscure rationales, definitions, and solutions to education-related issues. To the casual observer, these
elements may seem disconnected, but each piece actually affects the soundness of the whole educational system, as well as the wholeness of those who
work within a given school system. That stated, these elements have a major
impact on educators, parents, and students who share in the same system.

The five topics that have captured the attention of the American public in
recent years are testing, parent involvement, curriculum, educational change,
and bullying. These five elements remain in the public eye because they are
of varying degrees of importance—each in their own right. Additionally,
each carries with it a hefty price tag, as these hot-button issues create new
jobs, sell countless newspapers and books, and keep the focus off other
pertinent issues in education.

There are other educational issues that one would think deserve a constant
barrage of media headlines. However, they don't seem to have the same
sensational impact as topics such as bullying. Some of the topics that don't
seem to garner as much attention are: the mass expansion of special education in recent years; the correlation between diet and chemical exposure and
its effects on brain development in children; and the growing diabetes epi-
demic among children, which impacts health and overall wellness in children.

With each opinion and author's slant, educators, parents, students, and
community members remain in a constant state of confusion, known as a
*gray area.* Let us examine each of the five topics that the media keep in the
forefront. Those topics are testing, parent involvement, curriculum, educational change, and bullying.

## TESTING

Is the United States experiencing an identity crisis? The United States com-
pares itself to many Asian countries that excel in various academic areas. In
Asian cultures like China and Japan, scoring well on tests has long been a
primary goal. Testing is intended to bring clarity to learning. However, for
children and educators who grow up in a society like the United States,
which touts creative expression, the increase in testing is a conundrum.

Many educators have raised questions about the overtesting of children in
the United States. Testing in high volume may be suitable for some countries
and cultures, but for other cultures, like America, does its focus diminish the

creative capacity that American and other Western entrepreneurs have demonstrated over the past century?

Narrowing the focus, there have been many innovations in the last two decades born of American-educated individuals who drive industries in other countries today. For example, Travis Kalanick (inventor of Uber), Bill Gates (inventor of Microsoft), and Brandon Eich (inventor of JavaScript), all created innovations that have led to revolutionary changes in how business is conducted. Yet the fact that these homegrown individuals have shaped the direction of industries in the United States, as well as in other countries, gets overshadowed by the government, as government representatives continually publicize low test scores of American children in comparison to Asian countries.

Is this tactic meant to scare American parents into submission? A subsequent question might be: Is this news meant to control parents in a sense and direct the way in which they vote?

According to the *Washington Post* (Strauss, December 6, 2016), with regard to the 2015 Programme for International Student Assessment (PISA) test scores, the United States ranked fortieth in the world in math literacy (a drop from the previous PISA test rankings), ranked twenty-fifth in science, and twenty-fourth in reading literacy. In the current testing culture present in many U.S. schools today, if a political slant focuses on how poorly U.S. children are achieving, then this allows politicians, many of whom do not have a background in teaching and learning, to don a red cape and assure parents that they will save the day.

However, rolled into the PISA scores are several stories. There are tales of greed and corruption in inner-city school districts, as well as in rural school districts; unqualified leaders have been appointed by politicians in education at the federal, state, and local school district levels; and substandard school building conditions still exist in many school districts in the United States. And let's not forget the growing number of special education students in the United States. More testing in U.S. schools and random tweaking of school curricula won't solve the systemic problems. Politicians are not naïve to that fact.

After politicians have promised to fix education, the easiest way of camouflaging the fact that they know little about turning around schools is to identify some ills in education as well as people to blame, and continually keep the spotlight on the plight rather than on solutions. They become the presidential candidate who can point out the flaws in his opponent but can never outline a strategy to remedy the real problems.

Surprisingly, many politicians in modern-day politics have won elections employing that very tactic. While parents are in such a state of shock over the news about U.S. test scores as compared to other countries, they remain vulnerable to political rhetoric.

Western culture does not have the makeup of China, India, or Singapore. Cultures like that of the United States and the European Union (EU) can borrow elements from these countries in areas where they succeed education-ally, but we must also find our own equilibrium, combining those things that are unique to Western culture, such as individualism and creativity, and then tempering those elements with methodologies taken from efficient learning models found throughout the world.

Testing is not the sole answer to improving education in the United States, yet so much in U.S. education now weighs heavily on test results. Many of the countries that excel on tests in mathematics, technology, science, and reading have had a strong history of providing students with far more testing and test preparatory opportunities than their U.S. and some European counterparts.

Testing is ingrained in many Asian cultures, and along with that entrench-ment there are drawbacks. While Western culture has historically (until re-cent years) invested in the social underpinnings of children—building confi-dence and the imaginative side of children—children of Eastern cultures have typically been placed on specific career tracks for science, technology, the arts, etc., as a way of life.

For example, children in Japan have strong indicators as to whether they will be attending college by the time they are of high school age. Japanese children's futures are decided early in their educational career, primarily determined by test scores in junior high school. The *Japan Times* (Lewis, February 4, 2015) reported: "[M]any 14- or 15-year-old ninth-graders in Japan face the added pressure of knowing that their test results could affect their future employment options and economic prospects." The article went on to discuss the fact that mandatory education ends after ninth grade in the Japanese school system. That means that the Japanese government will not absorb the cost for students who cannot pass the entrance exam to secure a place in a public high school. "In most cases a student has only one chance to get into a public high school, where tuition is paid for by the government. If the student fails that test, their options are private school, night school, or correspondence school. The high school a young person attends can follow them around for life." The article further stated, "Young people who do not go to high school often join the workforce as unskilled laborers."

Nyak (2016), when writing about the Singapore educational system, stated: "However, there are concerns that this supercharged education system is too grades-focused and is taking the fun out of learning." The article went on to capture the feelings of children who were navigating the Singapore schools: "Another sixteen-year-old Tee Shao Cong said the stress in Singapore's education system was so intense that 'one's dreams could be shattered in a matter of seconds if we fail.'" To believe that your entire future rests on a test or tests at age sixteen is an extreme amount of pressure to place on a young person. Is this where the United States is headed?

Until recent years, Western culture has focused on cultivating a variety of aspects of a child—not placing so much emphasis on test taking. The United States is not China. However, just as there are aspects of Western culture that would fold nicely into Eastern culture, there are aspects of Eastern culture from which we can benefit.

As it relates to American testing and curriculum, the U.S. government generates proposed solutions that are designed to persuade schools and parents that specific initiatives will solve myriad problems in education. Politicians primarily use the PISA test results to make comparisons to other countries, and as a basis for framing arguments when the government desires to initiate educational changes.

The only solution to the present educational systems' pitfalls is symmetry. What the U.S. government has been most criticized for in recent years is that it rushes to support education initiatives before those initiatives have been tested to show significant improvement in American schools.

School systems across the United States are then put on a financial roller coaster, as with each major shift there are new financial obligations to meet. Even if state governments absorb some of the costs, still, that means state tax dollars are being spent on the back end. Local school districts lose money each time they are required to undergo a major change in education, while companies that create testing materials, supply new textbooks, and provide other necessary materials, increase their wealth. As well, politicians who invest in those companies, and the private interest groups who covertly market educational products, stand to gain.

Children profit from knowledgeable school staff, innovative approaches and methodologies, and the delivery of a quality education. Quality interactions throughout the school day with various staff members hold value for children, as they are all tangible living resources who are accessible to children on a consistent basis.

The frequent changes that students endure are questionable. While change is needed in education, children also require a level of consistency to thrive. Those who work with students daily often provide that stability. With rapid changes in curriculum and an increased focus on test-driven learning comes anxiety.

In the article "The Powerful Impact of Stress," posted on the Johns Hopkins School of Education website (education.jhu.edu), the author (Tennant, 2005) wrote, "Negative stress impedes learning, memory and performance." Tennant further stated, "Most of us can recall a time when the anxiety felt before a test, presentation, or other performance caused the mind to 'go blank' and all our studying and rehearsing went out the window. When the anxiety passes, information and skills come flooding back." Later in the article, Tennant quoted a researcher as stating, "When one is calm and alert the prefrontal lobes are free to engage in higher-level thinking tasks" (p. 85). It is for these reasons that countries that are in a current testing frenzy, and are haphazardly creating changes in schools, need to take a step back.

If U.S. schools are to benefit from testing initiatives, then the major decisions about testing must begin at the local school level, with professionals who know the students best. Otherwise, politics and greed stand to rob school districts of their right to provide a quality education and to make decisions about children in their individual communities. At the local level, children are faces, and not simply numbers. Therefore, the welfare and success of children in the local community will likely be top of mind for those who work closest with children.

Who puts in more hours with children over the course of their lives than parents? Getting and keeping parents involved in the work of educating children is paramount in improving any student's overall performance. A smart approach for schools is to find ways to support parents so that they can support their children's learning.

## PARENT INVOLVEMENT

In recent years, parents have become more actively aware of changes in education. This is largely attributed to the introduction of the controversial Common Core State Standards. The big question for school districts is: How do school districts harness all the parent attention that is now being paid to American school systems?

Creating platforms for parents to agree and disagree with curriculum changes establishes a sense of trust and makes parents partners in the education process in the truest sense of the word. Many schools feel compelled to "play defense" in response to parent pushback, but this only creates a dichotomy.

Parents have proven that they are savvy researchers regarding educational topics, and they have become loyal allies of school district educators in recent years. One only need examine Twitter, Pinterest, and other social media outlets as an indicator of growing parent interest—not only in local education matters, but in expanding their focus to encompass government involvement in education, as well. Furthermore, many parent comments posted on social media are hitting the mark.

For several reasons, learning institutions would not exist if it were not for parents, as parents are the cornerstone of schools. They financially support the school and community, and most importantly, they produce children—students who fill school hallways across the globe. When parents enter a school building, they are not guests—rather, they are a part of a school's fabric.

Principals and school superintendents often organize for parent pushback by preparing blanket responses to anticipated parent reactions. The most vicious cycle of dialogue between parents and school staff is when changes occur in education and parents ask the question: Why? School officials then respond with the following: "We are making changes because state officials told us to."

Why do schools often respond in this manner? Schools, like parents, often lack clarity as to why changes are necessary. Parents and educators deserve substantive answers. They need clarity, if for no other reason than to maintain an open line of clear communication with one another. If changes are speculative, then ultimately parents and educators land in a gray area.

How can parents and educators have a real voice in determining education initiatives? The smartest method of voicing an opinion is to put educational matters to a vote. That entails creating a referendum of sorts. At this moment in time, when parent interest and concern are at an all-time high, it would be easy to obtain the required signatures for referendums around educational matters. Major decisions such as the creation of charter schools, the choice to adopt any standards that are backed by the government, and the adoption of new summative statewide testing, could all appear as questions on state voting ballots.

In addition, education-related questions should be shared with schools, parents, and community members, at least two calendar years before proposed implementation, as the community ultimately absorbs the cost for professional development, new materials, and equipment associated with educational changes. This would allow parents, school leaders, and staff to conduct research regarding who is driving the changes, and what companies, if any, stand to profit from those changes. Parents and educators could have intelligent conversations, well in advance, about what is best for students at the local level.

School principals and teachers are easily accessible to parents and the community, so they feel the brunt of parent and community pushback. On the other hand, state and federal education officials are often viewed as obscure faceless entities that, ironically, have driven changes in education in recent years, but are a step removed from the immediate face-to-face dialogue with parents that occurs on the local level about mandated changes in education. This can cause strain on the parent-school relationship.

While parents are seeking answers to recent changes in education from school leaders, school leaders are seeking answers from the government. Oftentimes, neither are receiving answers that legitimize change. That is an indicator that there is a need for more local level input and control over curriculum and testing.

The response by parents to the implementation of the Common Core State Standards (CCSS) and the Partnership for Assessment of Readiness for College and Career (PARCC) in many states across the United States has been phenomenal. In terms of recent elevated parent interest in education, and parent involvement, it is a good time in U.S. education history. Sometimes a perfect storm is necessary in order for effective change to occur. Schools now have parents' full attention. How schools proceed in sustaining this parent interest will be a true test of school superintendents' and school principals' leadership skills.

It's hard to discuss the resurgence of parent voices in education without a focus on public school curriculum. Since curriculum in school districts became one of the hottest topics that recently prompted parents to take a closer look at what's really behind all the changes in education, it deserves to be examined. In particular, parents became extremely concerned at the direction of education in states that had adopted the Common Core Curriculum Standards. Even as some states are beginning to back away from the Common Core Curriculum Standards, there is still an abundance of public interest about education in the United States and what's next for public schools.

## CURRICULUM

The U.S. federal government supports the implementation of a common core curriculum for all American school systems. As it stands, the Common Core State Standards (CCSS) are not mandated by the government to be adopted by all school districts across the United States. However, if a state adopts both the CCSS along with one of its sister tests, for example, the Partnership for Assessment of Readiness for College (PARCC), which directly measures strands of the Common Core State Standards, then schools are forced to adhere to the CCSS.

Many state education officials are trying to defend their decision to adopt the CCSS by telling school educators and parents that this set of standards is flexible and is only a simple guide, and that school districts have a choice as to the degree to which they wish to implement components of the CCSS.

However, such statements are made contradictory when a state has adopted a measurement instrument such as the PARCC testing system, as the PARCC testing system was specifically designed to directly measure the common core standards. In a 2014 *Washington Post* article (Strauss, December 5, 2014), the following was reported: "After years of development and field testing and controversy, the new Common Core test known as PARCC is going prime time."

Why would any school district deviate from state-adopted curriculum standards when that state has also adopted a summative test that closely measures elements of those standards? It doesn't stand to reason, and this creates another gray zone for educators and parents, because fear is attached to deviating from the "norm," which is now known as the CCSS in many states, and is often reinforced by state and federal governments. At least that's how many educators and parents view recent curriculum standard changes, and with good reason.

Strauss (May 2, 2015), a writer for the *Washington Post*, titled an article: "Are Government Officials Trying to Intimidate Parents Who Resist Testing?" In the article, Strauss detailed that in 2015, approximately 200,000 students in the New York Public School system opted out of standardized testing, while in New Jersey that year, approximately 60,000 students opted out of PARCC testing. The article alluded to U.S. government intimidation by both the federal and state governments, as both threatened to withhold funds from school districts where opt-out numbers were high. The bottom line is that the testing was tied to the curriculum, that the government also supported—the CCSS. The two were a package deal.

Traditionally, states and school districts have developed their own curriculum standards. The first widespread discussion for states to have some level of cohesiveness as it relates to standards were World Class Standards, which didn't seem to agitate the majority of American parents and educators, unlike the CCSS has done in recent years. However, little did unsuspecting parents and educators know that the World Class Standards initiative would be the catalyst for ushering in the CCSS.

In 2008, a report was issued by the National Governors Association, the Council of Chief State School Officers, and Achieve, Inc. The report was entitled "Benchmarking for Success: Ensuring U.S. Students Receive a World-Class Education." Most educators and parents were already familiar with the term "world-class standards" by the time the report was produced at the turn of the century, in the early to mid-2000s, "World-class standards" for children in K–12 grades was a catchphrase among educators and parents who were looking to shape students who could compete worldwide while "preparing children for the twenty-first century." That catchphrase caught the attention of some Washington, DC, organizations.

This excerpt from that report was of particular interest: "In June, Harvard and Duke University researchers published the first in a series of studies documenting how corporations are no longer just outsourcing production, they are beginning to outsource innovation, as well.

"For example, big pharmaceutical companies such as Merk, Eli Lilly, and Johnson and Johnson are relying on India and China, not only for manufacturing and clinical trials, but also for advanced research and development. As a result, scientists are also increasing their ability to innovate and create their own intellectual property; the global share of pharmaceutical patent applications originating in India and China increased fourfold from 1995 to 2006."

Was this a result of poor education in the United States, or more a case of American-based companies investing in scientists abroad, seeking ways to curtail costs by shipping not only physical labor jobs overseas, but intellectual work, as well? The report was filled with comparisons about the booming economies in places like China and India, but left it to the reader to assume that much of our lack of "boom" in American industries was due to U.S.

children lagging behind educationally. The report became a perfect "fear factor" and would open the door to the development of the Common Core State Standards, which was supported by part of the same consortium—the National Governors Association and the Council of Chief State School Officers.

The detailed Common Core State Standards creates shades of gray for educators who wish to go beyond those standards and be creative in the delivery of instruction. After all, knowing how and when to inject creativity is often what separates a well-trained teacher from an individual who has no background in teaching methodologies. The well-developed educator can maximize resources, assess students, and make necessary changes with ease to ensure that learning is fluid.

Many parents and school systems view the Common Core Curriculum Standards as an intrusion of government, because typically in U.S. culture, "less" government involvement in education and other local matters is considered "more." Recently, to deflect attention from backroom politics, federal and state governments have focused on teachers' unions as a primary source of the "real problem" in education. Ironically, it is politics that has been the steady intrusion.

Teachers' unions did not gain noticeable latitude until the early to mid-1960s. In fact, the first state to pass a collective bargaining law for public employees was Wisconsin in 1959. According to the American Federation of Teachers (AFT) website, the United Federation of Teachers (UFT) was founded in 1960. Shortly thereafter, the UFT helped schoolteachers across the United States organize strikes and walkouts where working conditions were viewed as grossly unfair. These initial teacher strikes and walkouts took place between 1960 and 1965.

Contrary to what present-day government would have parents believe, teachers unions are not representative of the devil in education. Prior to the 1960s, there was plenty to be fixed in American schools. For example, in the 1950s, the well-respected media outlet, *Life* magazine printed a series that centered on educational topics termed "Crisis in Education."

That series included magazine covers with titles such as: "March 24, 1958—Exclusive Pictures of a Russian Schoolboy vs. His U.S. Counterpart" (questioning U.S. rigor in education); "March 31, 1958—Our Urgent Teacher Problem in Pay, Overwork, and Training"; and "April 1958—How the U.S. Wastes Its Gifted Children."

Over the past fifty years, there have been complaints, signs, and warnings that government was and would continue to be a major impediment to creating and sustaining a superb U.S. educational system. Let's face it, politics drives government. That leaves little room for true concern about the education of children. Government involvement has transformed from a supportive facilitating role in education to one that is more restrictive and has the hint of a dictatorship.

In an article that appeared in the *American Mercury* publication in 1958, writer William H. Allen wrote about what he believed was wrong with the New York public schools. One of the concerns he pointed out was what he viewed as a pay-to-play maneuvering of government. He dared to ask the question: How extensive was the search to find the best and most qualified person in 1958 to serve as the superintendent of schools—the highest post in the New York City Public School District?

Allen wrote: "For months and months the board of education advertised that it was 'scouring the nation' for the alert successor to Dr. Jansen [the outgoing superintendent of New York City Public Schools]. That scouring was a shoddy sham. Newspapers that pride themselves on uncovering top secrets of Washington, Moscow, and Wall Street couldn't find out who was being considered for the world's most foremost administrative post in education or what tests of superiority were being applied. When the sham 'scouring' ended, the nation's ablest was found in the mayor's deputy—as had all along been forecast by insiders."

The article went on to describe the qualifications of the mayor's deputy, who had been selected to be the incoming superintendent of public schools in NYC in the year 1958. Allen continued, "The new appointee had never been a teacher or administrator in a public school for a single day, much less for the five years that the law prescribed." Allen concluded, "For two years as deputy mayor, he had the power and sworn duty to bring about the correction of serious faults in the public schools. No corrections were cited." The lack of qualifications in school district leaders in K–12 public schools is a very familiar song that many educators and parents are becoming accustomed to today in U.S. public school districts.

So, in 1958, according to Allen, the New York City Board of Education appointed a former deputy mayor of New York City to serve as the superintendent of New York City's public school system. He had shown little signs of positively impacting the public-school district while in his role as deputy mayor. Yet, he was deemed perfect for the job as superintendent of schools, even though he did not meet the qualifications that were established by the state of New York.

Did he have the necessary knowledge and skills to strengthen or suggest specific changes to a school district's curriculum? This is an important question, because so many successes and failures of schools rest on the quality of a school district's curriculum. Thus, hiring a political appointee is likely not the best solution for selecting a superintendent of schools, especially if that person does not possess the proper teacher training or school administrative experience in education. (See chapter 11 for current examples of questionable appointments to high-profile education jobs in the United States.)

At various times throughout history, politics has played a role in shaping the direction of education. There were times when those interferences weren't all bad. In 1946, the U.S. Congress approved the National School Lunch Act. This created a basis for school lunch programs to be launched in school districts nationwide. In 1954 the U.S. Supreme Court heard the case of *Brown v. the Board of Education*—and ruled that segregated schooling in the United States was illegal. President Lyndon B. Johnson signed the Higher Education Act of 1965, which allowed more Americans access to colleges and universities.

Making political decisions based on the collective voices of local school districts and parents, and on their petitions to the government, was prudent. That is the essence of bottom-up change. However, the tides have slowly turned in the United States, and big government became more involved in local school district matters. The role of government has shifted over time, largely from the "facilitation of schools" to "authoritarian control." The major shift in government involvement in education came about in the late 1970s, when Jimmy Carter presided as president of the United States.

According to the United States Department of Education website, it was under President Jimmy Carter's administration that the U.S. Department of Education became a cabinet-level department. It had not been a part of a president's cabinet since the department initially lost its independent status in 1869. Instead, it had been a subdivision of the Department of Health, Education, and Welfare prior to the Carter administration. President Reagan, who succeeded Jimmy Carter in the presidency, had publicly stated he was against the U.S. Department of Education being a sepate executive department.

It was well known that Reagan was a proponent of less government oversight. However, Reagan did not follow through on his promise to detach the U.S. Department of Education from the presidential cabinet. Subsequently, education became a huge part of presidential political campaigns, and it remains a lively topic in political debates today.

Although President Carter believed that the U.S. Department of Education was necessary, even he expressed concern about the danger of too much government involvement in education decision-making, as he was quoted in an interview stating, "Another thing that concerns me very much is that we should have a concentrated commitment that even with the new department of education, that the Federal Government never gets into the role of trying to run the local school systems. That ought to be a decision made as closely as possible to the control of the parents themselves" (Administration of Jimmy Carter, September 23, 1978, p. 1611).

The math is easy. The majority of voters are parents and grandparents. Presumably, the adults in a child's life are concerned about the quality of education and the impact that education will have on a child's future. Given all the concern that is generated in U.S. families about the soundness of the country's educational system, education makes a good political platform for politicians, as it garners easy votes.

This is unfortunate for the American public, because most U.S. presidents cannot boast of having navigated teacher preparation coursework as part of their college training. Yet, because it can facilitate a political career, politicians promise improvements in education, and more specifically, presidential candidates feel compelled to make promises that relate to the advancement of the state of education. Present-day presidents are on a hamster wheel, and the American public is waiting for them to get off. Recent presidents have typically surrounded themselves with a small group of educational advisors (as compared to the vast educational systems across the world), and they proceed with a didactic plan for making changes in schools.

Of course, the plans will differ greatly from previous presidents' plans, especially if there is a political party change, *because another change is just what schools need.* The changes go into effect regardless of pushback from educators and parents. When a president or political leader doesn't know much about the grit of other political matters, education has become an easy "go-to." It can also be very lucrative for those putting the changes into effect, as there is insider knowledge of how education will shift, and that insider knowledge can be profitable to the individuals who are pushing changes through.

Some states, which recognize the slippery slope they have embarked upon by adopting the CCSS, now seek to change its name. The question to ask is this: Even though the name may change, are the underlying principles the same? Also, where is the apology to the school districts for all of the time and stress spent on implementing something that wasn't suited for a particular state in the first place? There is a great lesson here, in that foresight is worth a mint while hindsight leaves many districts financially and academically behind the eight ball.

What is alarming is the fact that the Common Core State Standards (CCSS)—the first real attempt for a countrywide curriculum in the United States—was never tested on a sample of students. According to education analyst Diane Ravitch (2013), "The standards unfortunately were never field tested. No one knew in advance whether they would improve achievement or depress it, whether they would widen or narrow the achievement gap among children of different races." Given this, the basic conclusion, then, is that the introduction of the CCSS to American schools was a shot in the dark. Why would one of the most revered nations in the world gamble with its children's education?

Is education the new Fort Knox? That is a question I posed in my first book, *Massaging the Mindset: An Intelligent Approach to Systemic Change in Education* (Nace, 2015). That question remains relevant. With a weakened economy, and the education market being a trillion-dollar "industry," are those in the business world looking to get their hands on what is often viewed as a pot of gold? What is driving the interest of those who wish to "privatize" education?

Suddenly, business men and women are applying to state governments to find ways to own charter schools. Once a charter school has been created, the money from the public school follows the child, and the owner of a charter school then controls that part of the public funds. However, there is not extensive research to suggest that charter schools can roll out a curriculum better than public schools. Despite this, it hasn't stopped charter schools from advertising that they will provide superior service to students. Why are parents, as a rule, not provided the right to vote on whether they desire to have a charter school in their community? Irrespective of the lack of long-term research, the federal government supports the increased development of charter schools.

Governments, (both federal and state) are so far removed from the day-to-day activities of schools that it is shameful for either to weigh in on curriculum without intensive input from local public school districts—not in hindsight, after implementation has begun, but instead when ideas at the federal and state levels are first being shaped. If not, then initiatives seem to have a shroud of secrecy attached and create a gray area for local school districts. Local districts are left with more questions than answers as it concerns what are often major changes in teaching and learning—the core of what they roll out each day.

This leads families and schools to distrust the motives of government. At a time when people are seeking transparency from government agencies, the expectation of the public is that there will be more inclusiveness of families and educators in policy-making, especially those policies that directly impact their children. Otherwise, government continues to create an "us-versus-them" dynamic with respect to the parent-school-government relationship.

## Chapter Two

# Educational Change and Bullying: More Gray Areas in Education

> Most of us spend too much time on what is urgent and not enough time on
> what is important. —Stephen R. Covey

This chapter continues the discussion from chapter 1 regarding five major focuses in education that have gripped the attention of parents, educators, and community members as of late. In the previous chapter, we examined three of the five major areas: testing, parent involvement, and curriculum. This chapter centers around two contemporary topics in education: educational change and bullying.

First, there is the burning question about how and when to create changes in schools. Then there is the concern about bullying among children—an almost-inescapable topic among parents, educators, and youth today. As it concerns these two topics, in this chapter, the reader will find suggestions for how to bring clarity to conversations surrounding these issues. Let us first examine educational change.

## EDUCATIONAL CHANGE

Schools continually ponder the best methods for implementing changes. When it comes to how to change effectively, admittedly school systems are some of the slowest institutions to change, and many are still fragmented in their methodologies. Disorganized movement keeps all who are involved in educational systems looking through an obtuse lens. Why? Because no single individual has the definitive answers in education.

However, many people each have a piece of the puzzle. That is why it is imperative that stakeholders work cohesively to bring about reasonable changes in schools. There are many changes occurring at an alarming rate in today's school districts, but to what end? Will those changes benefit children in the long term?

Changes best take shape when parents and educators, collectively, come to a consensus about what works most effectively for the children in their community. Also, a key to a successful change in a school district is when parents, educators, and community members know what their respective roles will be in the change process.

The pairing of parents and educators makes for a powerful dynamic as they move toward the same goals. Confusion sets in when changes occur too often and are not strategically planned. The bickering, bantering, and indecisiveness around whether to change, when to change, and how to change slow educational progress. Often students suffer in the interim.

Changes are rapidly occurring in education, especially within the last two decades, and the momentum does not appear to be on a decline. With the right planning, parents and educators can successfully navigate each development, as every change does have a silver lining. Change presents opportunity, but often one has to have the ability to recognize the diamond in the rough.

Professional experience has taught me that the key to effective change is to first identify potential benefits of a certain change and then find ways to leverage that change for the sole purpose of meeting one's desired goals. Much of education is about producing intelligent, healthy, giving, caring, and productive young people.

In thinking about many of the changes in recent years, basically, the fundamentals in education haven't changed, but ironically, there is an ongoing dialogue in education that gains momentum every few years, about how the fundamentals should be taught. Some new teaching and learning methodologies have actually created more confusion than clarity in classrooms and in children's homes.

When this occurs, yet another gray area is created for parents, educators, and children. A good example of this can be found in a *New York Times* article (Rich, 2014) that focused on new strategies that were implemented in schools across the United States as part of the Common Core Curriculum

Standards (CCSS). The piece detailed the frustration that parents felt when they attempted to help their young children with homework assignments.

Here is an excerpt from the article: "Ms. Nelam stated that she did not recognize the approaches her children ages, 7–10, were being asked to use on math worksheets." The article went on to state, "Her husband, who is a pipe designer for petroleum products at an engineering firm, once had to watch a YouTube video before he could help his fifth-grade son with his division homework."

This scenario speaks volumes about how much (if any) schools and parents have worked together to ensure that the parents were knowledgeable about major changes in the way a subject would be taught. It is clear from the article that there was likely a disconnect between the home and the school. This is a familiar story in many school systems, but it can be remedied with smart goals. How can parents and schools avoid similar traps?

## Tips for a Collective Approach to Change

- Parents and teachers should approach change as allies. Parents should note that there is no educational entity that has your child's best interest at heart like the local school district educators. State and federal governments may mandate changes from afar, but those who interact with children daily are more likely to know what works best in the classroom. Therefore, schools should incorporate parents in a real way, not just by engaging a core group that is agreeable, but by being creative in increasing the number of engaged parents who have varied opinions about educational topics.
- Parents and educators can conduct study groups collectively, as shared knowledge needs to be equivalent to a shared interest, which in this case is student success. Not only should schools provide workshops for parents, but collective book talks and discussions around educational articles can enhance and solidify parent-educator relationships. However, to remain clear of gray areas, educators who agree to engage in literature talks with parents should be mindful not to overuse educational jargon during such sessions. Using too much jargon is almost never viewed as impressive by parents.
- When collaborating on projects, there has to be mutual respect. Educators must be respected for their years of practice and ongoing learning in their respective roles as professionals. Parents, who see a different side of students and the community, bring a wealth of information to the table about

outside influences and the local environment. Each side must be viewed as an equal partner. The combination of two worlds that are so intricately connected can only enhance students' learning experiences.

- It would behoove leaders in school districts (school board members, superintendents, and school principals) to consistently nurture the relationship between school and home. Parents are major players in how smoothly change will take place in schools. Parents and school staff look toward school and district leaders to gauge how meaningful teacher-parent relationships are in the educational process. For example, school principals can request that office staff alert them when parents arrive to attend parent-teacher conferences. When principals take the time to briefly welcome parents, thank them for taking the time to meet with their child's teachers, and encourage parents to continue collaborating with school staff, this solidifies partnerships between home and school.
- There should be an established time frame in which all staff agrees to turn around parent phone calls and requests. Often, during times of educational change, parents will reach out to school professionals for clarity as they support their children in navigating these changes. The responsiveness of staff helps maintain a respectful partnership, and most parents will likely reciprocate the timely exchange of information.

As parents and school districts wrestle with changes in education, which all can expect will continually occur, there are many other issues that media and marketing gurus choose to keep in the forefront, and these issues stay on the minds of parents. Bullying is one such topic. One can hardly talk about change in schools without including some aspect of bullying.

Topics like bullying evoke immediate reactions from parents and educators, because people easily identify with it. Many remember what it was like to be teased as a child in school, and to say the least, it is a highly marketable topic. Has the simple act of teasing another child now graduated to bullying?

That question in itself is a gray area and deserves its own book. In fact, there are many gray areas associated with bullying. However, let us examine one side of bullying that is rarely observed.

## BULLYING

There are people who simply do not like one another. Regarding human nature, there is a gray area defined by feelings and emotions. Tension between individuals can occur at work, at play, in an organization, on a sports team, or in a family. What's puzzling is that, at times, people cannot pinpoint their dislike for another, but they know the dislike exists just the same. This is the work of humans—to strive for spiritual, emotional, and intellectual wholeness. Each situation presents a challenge to become a better human being.

With so much focus on bullying and those who bully in recent years, are schools unwittingly cultivating a gray area for all who come together to confront bullying behavior? Schools may need to take a step back, reflect, and make different choices.

Old tactics that are currently used to address bullying behavior have not made significant changes in bullying, as bullying behavior is still pervasive in many schools across the United States. According to the Centers for Disease Control (CDC), a 2016 survey of high school students found that 20 percent reported being bullied in the twelve-month period prior to the survey being conducted. This begs the question: Does the attention that bullies receive from school districts in the present day, actually fuel bullying activities?

In recent years, the Center for Disease Control has taken an interest in bullying, because according to the CDC's website, "Bullying can result in physical injury, social and emotional distress, and even death." There are health risks attached to bullying, and with those risks, rising concern. Why kids bully has generated more questions than answers.

## Gray Areas That Both Schools and Parents Would Be Smart to Consider about Bullying

- Spotlighting bullies can actually empower these individuals to continue their behavior. Coddling victims of bullying to the point that they feel comfortable in the role of victim, does more harm than good. When people fall victim to disempowerment, it leads to a cycle of repeated bullying. For example, the Los Angeles Police Department's website lists several reasons why women of domestic abuse remain with their partners. Here are a few that can also apply to any victim of abuse/bullying:

  1. Socialization creates a powerful inertia in relationships; people feel they must stay in a relationship and are highly resistant to change as a means of problem-solving.

2. Often the batterer is the only member of the victim's psychological support system, having systematically destroyed the victim's friendships.
3. Through learned helplessness, the victim has been taught and believes herself to be powerless.

- What is the percentage of shared culpability between the parent of a child who bullies and the bully? Once the school and community have established a set percentage, there is a level of expectation that the family unit will play an active and significant role in correcting a child's bullying behavior.
- Are there clear expectations outlined by the school and the local Parent Teacher Association (PTA) regarding the role of the parent of a bully? What are these parents expected to do in order to prevent their child from bullying others? Are there support systems/agencies in the community available to counsel these parents and children, and do schools readily have this information available to share with parents?
- Do schools utilize "reformed bullies" to act as mentors for other children, to prevent bullying behavior?

When schools have drawn a conclusion that an incident can be labeled as bullying, they tend to resort to a variety of strategies. Many schools have counselors on hand who deal specifically with bullying issues. Other techniques may involve conflict-resolution strategies. Principals often meet with students who are involved in the bullying incident(s) along with their parents to try to find a middle ground to resolve issues, and provide direction to students about policies and consequences.

However, these meetings can be viewed by the bully as a confirmation of his/her own power. The bullies set the agenda, because they essentially *are* the agenda. If it were not for the bully, then there would be no need for parents to rearrange their work schedules to attend such meetings, or for principals to arrange these conferences, and, of course, there would be no need for conflict resolution, which places the spotlight on the bully and often requires the victim to be present. These conferences require the victim to carve out time for such exercises.

As a bully peruses the room, he/she knows that the counselor, victim, principal, parents, and teachers have all been summoned because of his/her behavior. That can be invigorating to a child who bullies in order to gain attention and to feel powerful. While the school staff brings all of these individuals together to get a better handle on the situation at hand, staff may inadvertently be igniting the very flame they wish to douse.

## Disempowering Bullies and Corrective Action

- The bully's parents and the bully should be encouraged to take as much responsibility for stopping the bullying behavior as possible. This could be accomplished by the parent and child drawing up a contract with which the child promises to abide. This procedure will not interrupt the schedules of the victim or the victim's parents. The school and PTA can create a guide for developing such a contract. A school conference call, which includes the bully's parents, can initiate the task at hand. Let the family develop a plan of action—shifting the bulk of responsibility to the family unit, where the child's morals and behavior are first shaped and reinforced.
- Once school staff has a copy of the behavioral contract, the school should have an approval process in place, and then hold the child accountable to its contents, keeping in touch with the bully's family as the action plan rolls out. Allowing the family to take the initiative in creating the contract will provide schools some insight as to how seriously the family views the bullying behavior, and the school will also gain insight as to the family's behavioral parameters. If nothing else, the contract becomes a springboard for insightful conversations with family members. As it concerns bullying, without family insight, many schools are stabbing in the dark to find solutions.
- During the bully's recess period, before classes, or after school, the bully can prepare a written apology to the victim and then videotape the apology. It would be prudent for the school to create a general outline for writing the apology and for preparing the subsequent video. If done this way, the victims of the bully can view the apology at his/her convenience—meaning the victim's schedule is not defined by the bully; he or she would not have to be summoned to a meeting where the bully is present and is once again in control. If this process is consistently followed, then the bully feels the direct impact of self-inflicted inconvenience, as he/she would be required to generate a written apology and create the video during his/her free time, each time the individual initiates a bullying act.

- Cyberbullying could conceivably stand alone as a gray area in education. The Internet provides users with anonymity and therefore can be a dangerous tool for anyone, especially children—both on the receiving and sending ends of Internet use. Children are always testing the waters to determine what they can get away with—without getting caught. Every adult has stood in their shoes. In years past, it was stealing cookies from the cookie jar, then prank phone calls, and now it's making fun of others on social media. In terms of cyberbullying, this is where the parent-school relationship is crucial. When schools communicate with parents about cyberbullying, prevention is a major component to putting a stop to these acts. Once the messages are out in cyberspace, they circulate quickly and are difficult, if not impossible, to erase. So, getting ahead of these types of acts is crucial.

  1. Hold talks with students about the impact of cyberbullying on others. Use real-life "extreme" examples of how children can be driven to harm themselves because of such acts.
  2. Students should receive periodic information about cyberbullying—not just a one-and-done discussion at the beginning of the school year.
  3. Children should be aware of the consequences of breaking the laws surrounding cyberbullying. This is also a good time to share concrete examples of times when law enforcement became involved in related issues.
  4. Schools should outline to students the ways in which they can confidentially inform staff about cyberbullying incidents. This may prevent widespread circulation of damning information about a victim of a bully, and it can help schools and authorities identify cyberbullies before situations are no longer containable.

## CONCLUSION

Gray areas are created when individuals connected to school systems don't fully comprehend the intricate systemic threads that run throughout education. This requires all stakeholders to be reflective in order to gain a fresh perspective on how different parts of a system are intertwined. Testing, parent involvement, curriculum, educational change, and bullying are just a few of the elements that significantly impact various aspects of learning.

As you, the reader, will discover in other chapters of this book, there are a number of gray areas that create confusion among parents, educators, and children. The topics in this book that have been identified as gray areas are often thrust upon school districts by various governments in the form of laws, policies, or new initiatives. There is no exhaustive list of gray areas in education that can be created. That is because the elements of the learning process are infinite.

However, there are basic tangible connections that can be made in school systems. These connections become evident when educators and parents create visual representations that correlate to gray areas. The more parents and educators create visuals (such as charts, graphs, and other graphic organizers) that show the direct links of initiatives, strategies, teaching tools, and an array of other elements that impact learning, the more clear the vision becomes and the further away from gray areas schools can move. Take note of the example of a Systemic Impact Chart that shows how the five major gray areas identified in chapters 1 and 2 cross over into other areas and impact a school system.

**Table 2.1.   Systemic Impact Chart (1A)**

| How do the following elements impact school climate and culture, teaching and learning, and student outcomes? ↓ | School Climate and Culture | Teaching and Learning | Student Outcomes |
|---|---|---|---|
| **Curriculum** | If created effectively, curriculum has the ability to clearly define learning in the school setting and can induce a sense of calm. Equally, if the curriculum design is questionable, there is often top-down systemic confusion, especially if there was no staff input in its development. Whatever the overall consensus is about the quality of the curriculum, those feelings are then transferred to students and parents. | The quality of teaching and learning thrives with a reliable curriculum—one that staff and parents agree is rigorous, provides room for innovation, and prepares children for college, career, entrepreneurship, and life's challenges. | The curriculum reflects items that will be tested. Therefore, it is critical that the curriculum is designed in such a way that it helps students meet classroom expectations. The curriculum should be designed without borders, so that important elements that are often not reflected on summative tests, such as character building, verbal abilities, and social skills, become an intricate part of the child's learning experience. Also, these elements need to be tested in ways so that these skills are given the same importance to children as other subjects and skills that are currently the focus of summative tests in most K–12 schools. |

| How do the following elements impact school climate and culture, teaching and learning, and student outcomes? ↓ | School Climate and Culture | Teaching and Learning | Student Outcomes |
| --- | --- | --- | --- |
| **Testing** | The adults determine the climate and culture around testing in schools. Children will feed off the tension or calm of those administering the test. Also, parents play a significant role in ensuring that children are encouraged to do their best, and are in a sound mental state when they are set to undergo testing. | Collectively, educators and parents are charged with the task of ensuring that children are prepared for whatever assessments they face throughout the school year. That preparation takes place yearlong—it is woven into every lesson, discussion, cross-content subject area, and completed homework assignment. | When interpreted properly, testing outcomes provide a map for areas of improvement for students. Test scores also provide guidance for teachers and parents in how they should proceed in helping children set higher bars and achieve greater academic goals. |
| **Bullying** | Students need to feel safe. When a child is being bullied, he/she does not know what each day brings. There is uncertainty as to the extent that the individual will be bullied on any given day. A school that experiences high numbers of bullying incidents has a climate filled with tension, anxiety, and fear. | Because acts of harassment can cause anxiety, low self-esteem, and fear in students who are victims of bullying, it ultimately disrupts the teaching and learning process. Similarly, bullies, who put forth a great deal of energy intimidating others, often displace their academic efforts to do so, and they can fall short in their studies, as well. | Anytime students experience discomfort in a learning environment, there is always the likelihood that a distraction such as bullying can negatively impact student outcomes. |

| *How do the following elements impact school climate and culture, teaching and learning, and student outcomes?* ↓ | *School Climate and Culture* | *Teaching and Learning* | *Student Outcomes* |
|---|---|---|---|
| **Parent Participation** | The parent-school partnership helps to maintain balance in the school environment. Schools depend on parents to support learning in several ways. Parents play major roles in academic support as well as in fostering healthy social-emotional behavior. These elements directly impact school climate and culture. | The school often depends on parents to help children with homework assignments, to aid with special projects, and to ensure that necessary educational materials are secured. When parents take a positive and active role in education, classroom instruction then becomes an extension of the home. | When children know that parents and teachers are allied to guarantee their academic success, a feeling of security and support is generated. Students are then better equipped to meet learning goals. |
| **Educational Change** | Clarity is a major factor in how smoothly changes will take shape in schools. This is directly affects the school climate and culture, because sound reasons for change and clear messages provide both parents and educators with a sense of direction and purpose. | Teaching and learning thrives on effective change. Change keeps learning continuous and moving along a progressive trajectory. There is a science to change in education, which today is lacking, and this affects the quality of teaching and learning. Therefore, the reasons for initiating any change in education must be for the good of the children, and nothing more. | Regardless of the reasons for change, change will frequently occur in schools, and with each transition—whether positive or negative—student outcomes are directly impacted. |

*Chapter Three*

# What's It Like for Children in the Gray Zone?

Education is not the filling of a pail, but the lighting of a fire. —William B. Yeats

## THE GRAY ZONE

The term *critical thinking* evokes thoughts of light, vivid colors, creativity, energy, divergent thinking, and even infinity. There are no ceilings. When thinking creatively, a child is always "in the pink," so to speak—the place of all possibilities. These days, when one thinks of the current state of education, however, it is often associated with the color gray.

What's gray about education? The intense testing culture, the lack of morale among teachers to innovate, and students who are not even aware of the insufficient preparation they are receiving to navigate life. The nuts and bolts of how to successfully engage in adult life are not reflected on most K–12 educational tests.

So, how did the color gray first make its appearance in education? In 1983, the National Commission on Excellence in Education declared, "If an unfriendly foreign power had attempted to impose on America the mediocre educational performance that exists today, we might well have viewed it as an act of war." This statement was a wake-up call for the United States.

As educators and politicians began to reexamine educational systems across America, a primary focus became test scores. Increasingly, over the past three decades, producing high test scores has become the focus of educators at all levels—district, state, and federal levels government. This was a major indicator that American schools had entered a gray area.

Where is the focus now in education? Constantly testing students may create good test takers, but testing alone does not factor in all of a student's learning abilities. As schools spend a large percentage of time preparing students to take exams, other skill sets, like creativity, critical thinking, and the ability to construct, take a back seat to rigorous test preparation.

Who has time to develop children into true critical thinkers and innovators when so much in education now rides on test scores? The irony is that many of the tests taken that assess grade-level competencies are limiting, as they test very specific knowledge in a very narrow way. So, what do the results really tell parents and teachers about the abilities of children? Teachers, school administrators, and even parents in many school districts across the country are now programmed to drive students toward earning high test scores. One thing is certain: A child who repeatedly earns high test scores is a good test taker.

What message does this send to students? Does the amount of time focused on test preparation suggest to students that education is about the score, not the learning? What about those things that are not tested, such as social and emotional intelligence? These elements are not to be taken lightly, as they are the tools that will give children the ability to connect with others on a variety of levels.

In other words, how much time and emphasis is placed on those skills that will help children successfully plot a course in life? Not only do children need to possess the ability to get along with one another, but they need to be culturally savvy. This involves a process that goes beyond simply teaching children to be polite toward people whom that child may view as different.

When children possess knowledge of a variety of cultures, they become more desirable to most job markets. When a school district states that career readiness is one of its primary goals for children, diversity astuteness should be at the top of the list. Currently, how do schools accomplish this goal?

## LESSONS IN DIVERSITY

Children who land in a gray zone may become good at being politically correct, but do they really grasp the richness of cultures? One way to get kids out of this gray zone is through real relationship building. This is how people from many walks of life, over the centuries, came to understand one another.

It is a slower process than teaching political correctness, but it creates opportunities for thorough lessons in people appreciation.

Across the world, there are many types of relationships formed that consist of individuals from various backgrounds, who, for whatever reason, create a bond. For example, during the month of December, one can find many people whose dining room tables contain everything from Christmas cookies to potato latkes (a traditional Jewish food). Depending on that individual's circle of friends, the table spread will vary and be reflective of different cultures.

One may also attend religious ceremonies that are unlike their own, such as an Indian wedding, or a baptism, christening, or bar mitzvah, at the invitation of a friend or coworker. These types of invitations are openings for people to better understand different cultures.

Children will be invited to eclectic social events in their lifetime. Children don't have to stay in this gray area in education, especially if schools encompass cultural diversity in a meaningful way. One of the best returns on time spent in schools is the focus on creating intelligent young people who can evolve into contributing adults.

In other words, the phrase "development of children" does not translate to a "parrot effect" in the teaching and learning process. Children must have the opportunity to exercise thinking—to express true feelings, and question their thoughts about everything—even other cultures. That has always been the marvel of children—the ability to question. Simply telling children about other cultures may leave a lot of unanswered questions. Political correctness is very one-sided and leaves no room for dialogue about differences.

Presently, many children are given the appropriate responses to utter in what is deemed political correctness (P.C.). They no longer have to venture down the rabbit hole to discover the mysteries of people and life. Being P.C. takes care of all that.

As many towns now preserve open space for trees and other greenery to flourish, similarly there must remain room for children to be able to question popular opinion without the fear of social backlash.

If countries concentrate on providing a solid education for children as opposed to sharpening good test takers, then there would be no need for children to land in a gray zone, void of real opinions. The replacement of real opinions with political correctness has become a "fast-food" mentality that is sweeping across continents, as many societies seek quick solutions and results to growing cultural issues around the world.

Political correctness is a comfortable place for some school districts, because they can quickly check items such as "tolerance" and "diversity training" off the list and move on to the other hundred items that await their attention. In addition, if a school's sole purpose is to help students "pass the test," then there is no need to focus on building character, creativity, a variety of interests, or good decision-making skills. However, in doing so, children miss out on the wonderful interactions that quality learning experiences provide.

A better approach to teaching children about diversity is to replace the short lessons on diversity with lessons on systems thinking. Because we are all a part of one system—breathing the same air, having the same basic human needs, and often working together to accomplish goals—why not study how systems work? Systems thinking is the study of how people work and live together as a well-functioning system.

## LEARNING LIFE LESSONS THROUGH SYSTEMS THINKING

In *A Systems Analysis of Political Life* (1965), political systems theorist David Easton explored the *input > process > output* theory that unfolds in politics. Easton wrote about the impact that different groups have on politicians and the outcome of political decisions. He also discussed the widespread effects that each political decision has on society. The same theory can be applied to various aspects of life.

Every system has *inputs* (skill sets and knowledge that everyone brings into a system), a *process* (how skill sets are used in a given system), and an *output* (what the system produces). For example, if parents and schools can implement the study of systems thinking rather than provide fragmented lessons around bullying, diverse lifestyles, and individual cultural diversity issues, this can lead to better emotional intelligence in children.

Children need to understand how their actions impact a system. Through teaching lessons about how systems work, children can possess the ability to view every person as part of a wide, magnificent system. That understanding enhances critical thinking.

The social system in which we live is a man-made creation largely guided by religions, moral practices, and laws. The study of human beings as a system that works together to support future generations can lead children to have a better understanding of people, and thus lead to rewarding interactions. When people identify someone as being a "people person," it evokes good feelings. That's the type of person most people want to do business with and befriend.

On the contrary, subcategories of "race," such as black or white, tend to divide people. One example can be found in former third-grade teacher Jane Elliott's famous "Blue-eyes, Brown-eyes" experiment that she conducted with her third-grade class of all white students the day after the assassination of Dr. Martin Luther King Jr. in 1968. The popular exercise can be found on YouTube.

During this exercise, Elliott deliberately segregated the brown-eyed students in the class and the blue-eyed students. The students were made to believe that there was a learning difference between the brown-eyed and blue-eyed students. They were even instructed to drink from separate water fountains, and were given instructions that the brown-eyed and blue-eyed children were not to play together on the playground. She essentially segregated her class of all white students.

During the exercise, those who had been classroom friends prior to the exercise, turned against each other, and those who had once struggled with their studies were empowered by the title of being in the superior group, and the teacher noted a rise in their grades. Additionally, those who were once advanced learners began to struggle with their studies when they were labeled as part of the inferior group.

The Blue-eyes, Brown-eyes experiment demonstrated the damage that labels can cause to children and the devastating effects it can have on both their confidence and learning outcomes. Often children see themselves through the eyes of the adults in their lives. Therefore, careful attention needs to be paid to how adults view children and interact with them.

Jane Elliott, being a teacher and not a psychiatrist, did not consider some of the ill effects that the experiment might ultimately have on very young students. However, as seen in the documentary, her class emerged with life-long cultural lessons about the impact that one's perceptions and bigotry can have on another. Fast-forward to the present day, and still societies are plagued with the polarization of cultures and communities. So, what solution befits a modern world?

There are many cultures that express the desire to create cohesive relationships among people of varied backgrounds, but there is work involved in moving past the belief that geography alone is half the battle. By that, I mean, when different cultures share the same space—community, work, school, or country—there is an assumption by some that proximity alone can cure cultural divides.

Buckley (1966), a former candidate for mayor of New York City, wrote in a position paper: "The purpose of education is to educate, not to promote a synthetic integration by numerically balancing ethnic groups in the classroom. In today's all-white neighborhoods, it is reasonable that the schools should be overwhelmingly white. In today's Negro neighborhoods, it is reasonable that they should be overwhelmingly black. Mature, self-confident, and mutually respectful relations between the races are more a by-product of sound moral education than the automatic results of integrated schools, and the integration of neighborhoods."

Still, in 2018, there is ethnic unrest around the world. The obvious is overlooked. The answer is not found in thrusting children together or teaching them simply to be polite toward one another. The real work lies in teaching children that belonging to a society brings with it a responsibility.

There is a human system at work that is often studied in fragments and is rarely discussed. For the most part, the media and the general public talk about problems in an isolated way—not always connecting one problem to another. Making the world and everything in it make sense—that's where systems thinking comes into play for children in the classroom as well as at home.

## SYSTEMS THINKING, THE VALUE OF LIFE, AND COLLEGE AND CAREER READINESS

Regardless of the girth of a house or how shiny a new car might be, it is prudent that human life be viewed as the most valuable asset by children. Otherwise, we as a society lose our purpose. There are some disturbing trends occurring around the world that inevitably affect children in this regard.

Hatmaker (2012) made some profound statements in her book *7: An Experimental Mutiny against Excess*. When discussing what she describes as the "excess machine," she suggests that many people are trapped in a cycle of overspending and overconsumption. Hatmaker stated: "It's time to admit I'm trapped in the machine, held by my own selfishness. It's time to face our spending and call it what it is: a travesty . . . so many areas out of control. . . . What have we been eating? What are we doing? What have we been buying? What are we wasting? What are we missing?"

The latter question in her moment of self-reflection is of real importance to children—the next generation. What will be their inheritance—to pick up where the current generation leaves off? With consumption and social media as the primary anchors for many children, the web of overspending has already been woven. What will they value most?

The Federal Bureau of Investigation (FBI) defines "mass shooting" as the shooting of four or more people. According to a *PBS NewsHour* article (2015), in the United States alone, by the close of the year 2015, there had been 372 mass shootings in that twelve-month period, killing 475 people. According to the Center for Disease Control (CDC), in 2014, 9,967 people were killed in drunk-driving accidents. Also, the CDC reported that in 2012, there were 699,202 abortions performed in the United States.

How do children digest acts that seem to reject the notion that human connections are important? Through their young eyes, how do they perceive the value of life? Having the ability to think critically plays a major role in sustaining a thriving humanity. Children's mind-sets and worldviews also influence learning.

Are adults inadvertently teaching children to value commodities over people? If so, what will be the implications? As schools gear up to prepare children for college and career readiness, how will they enter the workforce? What depth will they add to college and university conversations?

As we know, testing has become the most important single factor in the United States when determining whether children are college and career ready. Yet, thinking systemically is likely not to be found on any of the many tests that students will be required to take while at in their K–12 grade levels. However, the average job requires teamwork these days. Are schools properly preparing children to meet that demand?

The typical summative test (taken at the end of each school year) does not incorporate or assess the attributes that make a young person personable, honest, a hard worker, and a reliable colleague. Young people grow up to be adults who will either make good and fair choices based on each unique experience with each person they meet, or they will make decisions based on something trite like skin color, the way an individual is dressed, the car that someone drives, or any of a number of other trivial factors.

Working collectively with others is a skill that requires more than a few training sessions on the job. It begins when children are young, and then those skills are sharpened and applied in their adult lives. Learning to work successfully as a group or, more precisely, as a system, is acquired learning.

In other words, it takes time to build the necessary foundation to appreciate what others bring to the table, and to know how to use others' skill sets to complement your own. It also requires learning to know when it is beneficial to be a "chief" and when and how to be an "Indian" when engaged in teamwork.

Whether children choose to become police officers or scientists, decision-making, how well they work with others, and their basis for making choices will certainly drive their effectiveness on any job once they become adults. Thinking about others in a systemic way can help children become more effective in their adult lives.

What are the ultimate goals of all of us—as humans? One goal that most would agree upon is ensuring the survival of the human race. Most importantly, we need to understand that survival is endangered by the polarization of people, and the poor education of children. Coupling systems thinking with independent creative thinking can create the right balance for preparing children for teamwork in the classroom as well as in other aspects of life.

As children embark on college and career, how they value other humans will impact their relationships and their effectiveness in higher learning institutions and their careers as they interface with fellow students, professors, and colleagues from a variety of cultures. How does the violence (input) that children directly or indirectly encounter each day through different media sources affect their learning and interactions with others (output)?

Around the world, gang violence in various forms is prevalent, terrorist attacks and terrorist threats abound, and senseless mass shootings occur on a regular basis. In addition, there is always a war somewhere in the world. With all of the killing of humans occurring at an alarming rate around the world, is it safe to assume that the killing of a fellow human being has become commonplace in society?

If so, again, what effect does this have on a young mind? Students who learn about systems thinking from an early age can understand how the human social system works and why it is imperative to respect all life. This stands in sharp contrast to the reports of killings that they are bombarded with in the media each day. The study of systems could create a much-needed balance for today's children, who are exposed to a seemingly disconnected society, as evidenced by a stream of violence showcased through a variety of media outlets.

There are simple lessons around systems thinking, such as: Whatever one puts into a system, whether negative or positive, will be a part of that system's outcome. When children understand and respect how systems work (the inputs and outputs in life), they also learn to have regard for various cultures and lifestyles as they learn that everyone contributes to the input as well as the output, and are therefore significant.

It is imperative that children understand that we don't all need to earn the same salary, dress in the same manner, or share the same viewpoints or religion—but it is necessary to understand some fundamental common goals of human survival. There are more human elements than not that connect those in a society. The connectedness of things around us is a principle found in many engineering courses. However, many schools do not teach from a "connected" perspective.

These are easy lessons to teach, as people generally have a desire to feel linked and connected to one another. The explosion of social media is a good example of that. However, when children are taught to be politically correct at all times, there is no room for opinion. To be a critical thinker, one must first possess the ability to discuss issues at length. Every person deserves that right.

While political correctness provides a temporary solution to the "me" versus "we" problems in society, it is not enough to simply tell children to be politically correct at all times. There must be some reasoning behind it. Otherwise, children's polite responses to people and situations are just that— knee-jerk reactions.

## JUST HOW IMPORTANT IS EVERYONE?

Each person plays a significant role in keeping the human social system moving forward. Take a cell phone, for example; the actual phone is no more important than the battery that keeps it energized. The same holds true for people, as each person's role in life has immeasurable worth.

A child studying systems thinking might eventually ask: What about criminals? Do they play an important role in society? According to *The Federal Registry: The Daily Journal of the United States Government* (2015), the average cost per year to house each prisoner in federal prison in the United States, in 2014, totaled $30,619.85 per inmate. This is another concrete example that each one of our actions affects the whole system.

The prison system creates a plethora of jobs—the companies that supply the sheets, food, canteen items, and even the local electric and gas companies all benefit from the existence of these institutions. There are some people whose crimes are so heinous that they need to be imprisoned. There are also many minor offenses that land people in prison, and as a result, generate business opportunities for companies who bid to supply items to prisons, as is the process in many U.S. prison systems.

The legal system is massive, and it generates financial resources for many states. It is also a large employer, employing prosecutors, parole officers, corrections officers, judges, court clerks, and an abundance of administrators. Because America no longer manufactures a great deal of products and because so many manufacturing jobs have been shipped overseas, it is not uncommon for some states to step up their efforts to generate revenue in this area. Students can study the relationship between a decrease in one aspect of society and an increase in others.

For example, *USA Today* posted an article entitled "Red-light Cameras Generate Revenue, Controversy." There are red-light cameras across the United States taking photos of license plates when drivers are believed to have run a red light. However, some citizens and politicians argue that the red-light cameras were put in place, not for safety reasons, but instead to generate money for various states and townships. In the state of Florida alone, drivers who were caught by red-light cameras paid more than 100 million dollars in traffic fines in 2014.

When students are given opportunities to figure out why problems arise in different systems—not just asked to read news articles about countless concerns and problems in society—and really pull them apart and investigate why changes occur, then they journey down the road of systems thinking. They don't simply take news and world events at face value. Children begin to understand the direct effects that systems have on various people, as well as themselves.

This is known as cause and effect. It is a simple lesson that children learn in elementary school that can easily be expounded upon as children grow older. Particularly with news stories in the media, cause and effect usually involves a shift in one system that impacts another. However, those cause-and-effect relationships are not always readily apparent to children and will take some practice in critical thinking, encouraged by a parent or teacher.

Regarding the red-light cameras, Jeff Brandes, a St. Petersburg Republican, is quoted in the article as saying, "Three years ago these red-light cameras were pitched as safety devices. Instead, they've been a backdoor tax increase." A 2012 audit in St. Petersburg, Florida, showed that the number of rear-end collisions increased at intersections where red-light cameras were posted.

The audit concluded that many drivers stopped short at these red lights, which caused them to rear-end other's cars to avoid violations and the dollar amount they would have to pay. Additionally, research from the Texas A&M Transportation Department also showed a spike in rear-end collisions at intersections where the red-light cameras were installed in cities around Texas. These facts would make for great cause-and-effect conversations with students.

Countless newspapers across the United States published articles about the installation of red-light cameras. When the articles first appeared, they announced the installation of red-light cameras by touting how they would help stop drivers from running red lights and decrease accidents at intersections. At that time, children could have been asked what they believed was the cause and the effect of the installation of the cameras in their respective townships.

Regardless of what the newspapers or other media outlets state, kids should regularly practice forming their own opinions. Asking how these cameras would impact systems would have been a great strategy, because this could have led some children to predict a possible rise in accidents at intersections where the cameras had been installed.

Children are very creative, and they often surprise adults with their connections and responses, when they are provided with a free-range learning environment. It is in the spontaneity, not the scripted lesson, that some of the best learning moments will happen. That is when teachers and parents can draw good critical thinking from children.

The article went on to state: "[R]esistance to red-light cameras may be growing. Nine states already prohibit them, and lawmakers in Ohio are considering a ban, even though the cameras generated 16 million dollars for Ohio cities [in 2014]." Brandes stated, "The state shouldn't be counting on people to violate laws in order to pad their budgets."

In instances like this, children could study the downfall of one system (such as the steep decline of factories and other industries in the United States) and its effects on other U.S. systems (such as the legal system)—for example, taking a closer look at the red-light cameras that have cropped up in large numbers across the United States. The study of systems can evoke good critical thinking in children, as there are many systems to examine and compare.

How does one begin to study systems thinking? It's not rocket science, but it is in large part how rockets are built. There is hardly anything that a person encounters that doesn't have a system attached to it. For example, students who study engineering study all types of systems and how they work to produce a certain outcome or product. However, all of us encounter systems all the time, so the study of systems thinking is appropriate for people of all ages and grade levels.

Students in K–12 grades can begin to study systems thinking by observing the many different types of systems there are around them—both natural and man-made. That study could include the following: political systems, ecosystems, transportation systems, mechanical systems (motor vehicle designs, for example), sewage systems, the solar system, and the human body which is a phenomenal system, just to name a few.

## HOW TO STUDY SYSTEMS

By studying systems and how they operate, children will come to understand themselves and their effect on the world and the people in it. There are so many lessons to be learned in observing the complex and simple principles that are found in systems. The study of how things work (the input, process, and output) is at the root of every innovative plan and design. When creating plans, one should keep in mind: What are my desired goals/outcomes?

That person must also consider the step-by-step details and processes that need to take place to reach set goals. Once the goal is reached, how will that outcome affect other parts of a system? In other words, once goals are achieved, that achievement will always change the dynamic of a school, family, or organization. These are basic principles from which any young learner can benefit.

When we look at human life as a large system, there are all types of roles that people play to support the system. Sometimes a child's contribution can be as simple as drawing from his/her own past mistakes and teaching others from that point of view. A valuable lesson for children to learn is that people who have overcome hardships firsthand can provide immeasurable insight to others and should not be discounted. They add something important to systems. That makes for a meaningful, lifelong lesson.

Another great lifelong lesson around systems thinking can be found in Carnegie's (1998) book *How to Win Friends and Influence People*. In the book, Carnegie suggested that people all want to feel important and we only need to find the positives in others to begin to engage them in positive ways. In other words, he suggested that people be interested in someone other than themselves—not just in one's own personal life and needs—and this will open the door to communication and relationship building. He discussed the positive effects of being connected to others. However, rarely are such systemic skill sets discussed in classrooms or measured on K–12 tests.

An important and simple lesson for children to learn would be that when people are disconnected, they tend to trivialize others. For example, those who stand in judgment of others are likely to feel superior to the individuals on whom they pass judgment. They cannot see the similarities. Only the differences drive their desire to dominate, ridicule, and demean another person.

Contrary to what some may believe, systems thinking is not a lesson in socialism. Rather, children maintain their competitiveness and individuality but have a conscious understanding of the links that run throughout society. They engage in learning about how people and things work together to achieve favorable results. How children apply those lessons should be left up to them.

## CONCLUSION: BEING CONNECTED

Across the world, teachers and parents desire that kids become good team players, yet many do not teach children how a well-run system works. Teamwork is a collective effort, and children engage in teamwork all the time. For example, children coordinate with others as a part of sports teams, during social play, and in classrooms where they are often asked to complete assignments in small groups, or "teams."

Essentially, what educators and parents expect of children is that they will think and work as a system. However, how often do adults ensure that children understand the concepts behind working as an efficient team/system?

Here are a few major concepts to consider:

- To become an effective team, the team has to first understand how a well-run system works.
- Teamwork happens even when one is alone. What a person does in private can often impact another's life. Those actions will have a ripple effect somewhere down the line. In other words, people can impact a system, even when working alone.

- Each person contributes to the input, process, and output in a system. These terms should be defined for children in age-appropriate definitions prior to children being asked to work in teams.
- Every person is a part of the whole system. Therefore, each person impacts the system. For example, CEOs of companies can impact a country's overall economic system just as much as homeless people do. Perhaps, each will not impact a system in the same way, but each group's impact will alter the system.
- All actions are significant. Even people who like to sit on the sidelines and do "nothing" will impact a system. They likely have valuable skill sets that could be used to enhance a system, but they may choose not to use them. That action, too, has an important impact.
- Before there is a motion, there is first a thought. That is why it is important to study and understand systems thinking before entering into a team situation. The child's mind-set should be ready to think and work as a team.

Preparing children to successfully navigate life and understand the people they will ultimately interact with is a worthwhile endeavor. However, it takes layering of knowledge to achieve, and students will need several real-life projects and experiences to truly understand how human systems, social and otherwise, are interconnected, and what role they play in those systems. When we understand the whole that links each individual, then everything—from work to raising a family—becomes more meaningful.

In former U.S. Secretary of State Condoleezza Rice's book *Democracy* (2017), she had this to say: "[T]he trend toward dividing people into ever-smaller groups, each with its own narrative, comes at the expense of the unifying identity that all democracies need. This is especially true in the United States, where 'we the people' has no ethnic, national, or religious basis. We reinforce those divisions at our peril" (442).

If we want children to have a deeper understanding of what it means to be "connected," then we may need to reconsider how schools and parents teach diversity lessons. As it stands, "connected" these days generally mean to be on social media or surfing the Internet. There are many important meanings of "connected" that children can explore, such as thinking of themselves as being linked to one another, and thinking about the impact that the manner to which they relate to the world and the words they speak have on other people.

Children are ultimately expected to enter the workforce and work with others as a cooperative team. However, not all of them will ever really consider and appreciate the intricate design and balance of working as a system with their colleagues on a daily basis, unless they are made aware of the impact they have on others. Naturally, children entering the workforce will be highly interested in their earning power.

The average adult drives to work each day focused on things like whether they will encounter traffic, whether they will have time to stop by their favorite convenience store to get a cup of coffee, or how many e-mails await them at the office. A more useful approach to starting the day would be to consider what they will put into the system (their workplace) that day, and how their contributions will affect the company or organization for which they work. Children can begin thinking systemically in schools and at home as they consider their role in the world and the impact they have on the people and places around them.

Children have the intellect and capacity to evolve at an accelerated rate if they can learn to look at the world as a series of systems. Schools and parents have the opportunity to make our future workforce better. Systems thinking could be a solution to teaching about cultural differences and the worth of others, irrespective of religious, cultural, or lifestyle differences. Systems thinking focuses on the end goals and the contributions of all.

*Chapter Four*

# Religion: The Light of the World

For physical training is of some value, but godliness has value for all things.
—1 Timothy 4:8

IS THERE A PLACE FOR RELIGION IN SCHOOLS?

Do schools support and build on the natural strengths of children? Children possess the gift of innocence, they have the natural ability to use their imaginations, and they have blind confidence in the adults around them. Children trust that the adults in their lives will make sound decisions concerning the quality of their education.

One notable example of controversy about the quality of a school district curriculum arose in the 1920s. The courtroom struggle to introduce the theory of evolution into American classrooms came to be coined the "Monkey Trial" of 1929 (see *Encyclopedia Britannica*, https://www.britannica.com/event/Scopes-Trial). As the case was unfolding in an overcrowded courtroom, many believed that the very act of thinking was on trial. Eventually, Darwin's theory of the evolution of man became a part of some curricula across the United States, but the implementation was a tough sell and it took decades to achieve. And in places where Darwin's theory was taught, it was presented as a hypothesis—not a fact.

It is also noteworthy to add that to utter a word about religion in American classrooms between the 1920s through the 1960s was not frowned upon, but neither was it commonplace for teachers and students to stand up

45

on a soapbox and suddenly begin preaching the gospel in classrooms. Religion was not a disruption to the learning process.

Why are some elements of the instructional day preempted while others are injected into classroom culture? In non-divisive ways, at times religion added much to classroom discussions. Do children of today miss out on the study of a vast part of human culture?

The National Education Association (NEA) published a set of guidelines. They are designed for educators to understand facets of appropriate religious expression in schools. Also, the document provides guidance on how to incorporate religion into instruction across the curriculum.

The guidelines state: "Understanding art, music, drama, history, literature, and current events requires an understanding of religion's influence. Instruction must be objective and neutral, so that students gain awareness, but are not pressed to practice or favor any particular faith tradition." However, with so many oversensitive reactions by parents to religion in schools, many teachers are afraid to incorporate religion into the school day.

In a *New York Times* article entitled "Blending Religion into the Curriculum," Briggs (1984) interviewed Professor Charles Knicker of Iowa State University. Briggs questioned why religion was not widely incorporated into classroom lessons. Knicker responded in part by saying, "there is the fear of controversy. As the old saying in education goes, when in doubt, leave it out."

For every gain, there is a loss. The quick-fix trend of "acceptance of all" is reinforced pretty much everywhere in today's society. When schools decide to introduce or reintroduce new areas of learning into a curriculum, there must be thorough training of educators. When educators are well-versed about new topics, they feel comfortable and can teach in a way that is meaningful and not harmful or confusing to children.

The *New York Daily News* (Garcia, 2011) reported that students were reprimanded for uttering "God bless you" after a fellow student sneezed in class. The incident took place in Vacaville, California. According to the article, "a health teacher at William C. Wood High School decided to deduct 25 points off students' grades if they say the phrase during class, reported Fox40 Sacramento." One parent, Alan Johnson, was quoted as saying, "I think that's ridiculous. First, the Pledge of Allegiance, now preventing a kid from saying, 'Bless you'?"

Up until the early 1990s, many children and adults would likely offer an array of responses to questions about religion, culture, and sexuality. Now, post the introduction of political correctness, and almost instinctively, children are silenced about their religion, as many schools insist that children should "leave their religion at the school door." Yet, on the other hand, schools focus much of their attention on improving school culture and school climate. Isn't that where religion can play a positive role?

Many religions teach children basic principles about how to treat others and how to navigate the world in which they live. Included in many religious teachings are lessons about conduct, honor, and best practices for living a wholesome life. When schools expect children to "disrobe" and check their religion at the door, one could argue that this is a form of religious persecution.

Schools herd children toward accomplishing goals, but which goals get nurtured? Without some acknowledgment of religion, how fulfilling will those goals be to children? Do young people of today equate success with the acquisition of things?

As far back as the 1980s, there were those who were concerned about the direction of future generations and how they would perceive success. Stephen Covey (1989), author of *The 7 Habits of Highly Effective People*, described what he termed "Possession Centeredness" as: "If my sense of security lies in my reputation or in the things I have, my life will be in a constant state of threat and jeopardy that these possessions may be lost or stolen or devalued. If I'm in the presence of someone of greater net worth or fame or status, I feel inferior. If I'm in the presence of someone of lesser net worth or fame or status, I feel superior. My sense of self-worth constantly fluctuates. I don't have any sense of constancy or anchorage or persistent selfhood. I am constantly trying to protect and insure my assets, properties, securities, position, or reputation. We have all heard stories of people committing suicide after losing their fortunes in significant stock decline or their fame in a political reversal."

Defining success by material surroundings is commonplace in society. Do schools inadvertently teach children that this is the goal? While religion offers children a different type of anchor, it is typically shunned in schools.

That is not to say that consumerism isn't important, but materialism tends to keep the mind on less practical matters. Let's face it, consumerism keeps currency fluid in societies, helps businesses thrive, and when thriving businesses move into a community, that can help keep property taxes low. "Materialism" is defined as "a preoccupation with or stress upon material rather than intellectual or spiritual things" (*Merriam-Webster Dictionary*, https://www.merriam-webster.com/dictionary/materialism).

Conversely, religion can be a useful vessel for centering children, and can add depth to what they value in life. The lure, and often, trap of materialism is virtually inescapable. However, even in the whirlwind of consuming, one can find balance in the nurturing of the spirit.

What runs through the mind of a child who is taught that by all rights religion is good—an idea reinforced by family and religious leaders—but who has had religion excluded from a large part of his/her day, in a public facility that is largely supported by community tax dollars? This can be confusing to a child, but oh well; it's just another gray area to which kids become accustomed.

In terms of school staff and their religious backgrounds, there is no need for staff to stand on their respective soapboxes and profess their religion to the world, but aren't they people, too? Many teachers have very rich cultural backgrounds and histories. The mere mention of their religion would likely not be harmful to children. In fact, it could prove to create a rich realistic learning environment in schools. It could also help children identify with elements of life that are important, elements other than material possessions.

School as a true microcosm of society can be a more enriching place—representative of the world in which children will navigate as adults—filled with people who cling to some form of religious belief. However, striking the appropriate balance takes the proper training of school staff, and that's where many schools fail.

## PARANOIA AND RELIGION IN TODAY'S SCHOOLS

There are teachers who honestly believe they must not mention religion in the classroom—ever. This is simply not true. Why are most teachers not privy to their rights? Many school leaders encourage teachers to adopt a zero-tolerance policy for religious discussion in classrooms. Principals who encourage this behavior, however, do this primarily for risk-management purposes—not necessarily in the best interest of the children.

Without the proper training regarding their rights, educators almost always completely steer clear of any conversations involving religion, and children miss out on what could very well be informative and engaging exchanges with their teachers and peers. This is what many adults enjoy today—a free exchange of ideas about their religion, their cultural differences, and their likes and dislikes among close friends and within comfortable social circles. These are some of the same conversations that parents likely discussed with their own teachers at one time or another.

However, today, even adults are finding it difficult to voice honest opinions in mixed company. The typical child of today, if asked about cultures and lifestyles, cannot offer in-depth opinions. There is a stigma in public schools attached to openly discussing religion, and there are modern reflex answers to hot-button topics—better known as politically correct responses.

Some children, those who have a strong desire to fit into their young social circles, would rather avoid religious discussions altogether, and even turn from religion instead of running the risk of being ridiculed by their peers or silenced by the school staff. School staff members likely do not set out to impede children who initiate religious references, but staff will not engage children in this direction because they are often afraid of potential repercussions.

In Santa Rosa, Texas, a teacher was allegedly reprimanded for talking about God in the classroom. CBS4 reported, "Administrators spoke with math teacher Charles Zeissel last week, said Superintendent Heriberto Villarreal. District policy forbids instructors from talking about God in the classroom." In response to Zeissel's reprimand, the news outlet stated, "[Students] protested on Monday, holding signs that read 'If speaking the word of God is wrong, I don't want to be right' and 'Freedom of Religion.'"

In a separate incident, in Phillipsburg, New Jersey, a substitute teacher gave a Bible to a student upon the student's request. He was fired for this action. Fox News (2017) reported that the substitute teacher, Walt Tutka, was later rehired by the school district, writing, "It did not seem to matter to the school district that the student had asked for a copy of the Good Book. [The organization] First Liberty Institute took on Mr. Tutka's case—and eventually scored a victory with the Equal Opportunity Commission. They agreed that the school district had discriminated against Mr. Tutka on the 'basis of religion and retaliation.'"

Learning the art of how to legally and seamlessly incorporate religion into classroom discussion adds another dimension to classroom interactions. Facilitating children in the art of conversation—teaching them not to necessarily win a religious argument in classrooms, but rather, use some aspects of religion to strengthen a nonreligious argument at play—can reinforce the ability of children to form effective arguments and think critically.

There are circumstances in which teachers are protected by law and there are guidelines they must follow, but teachers can legally mention religion in the classroom and, to some degree, children can inject religion into classroom discussions.

On the other hand, teachers cannot preach religious rhetoric to children, as that is where the danger arises. Schools are leaning toward quick solutions in reaction to court decisions such as the landmark case *Engel v. Vitale* (1962), which basically made it illegal for school officials to compose an official school prayer. This ruling sent waves of reservation throughout school districts as to what was permissible regarding prayer and religion in schools. There remains a vast opening here regarding how schools can legally include prayer, religious discussions, and elements of religion into the school day.

According to the First Amendment Center website (www.firstamendmentcenter.org) involving a 1963 case "In *Abington v. Schempp*," Tom Clark wrote for the court: "[I]t might well be said that one's education is not complete without a study of comparative religion or the history of religion and its relationship to the advancement of civilization. It certainly may be said that the Bible is worthy of study for its literary and historic qualities. Nothing we have said here indicates that such study of the Bible or of religion, when presented objectively as part of a secular program of education, may not be affected consistently with the First Amendment."

There are school principals who understand certain ethics around religion and education but choose not to ensure that teachers know their rights and boundaries, thus they simply ban or strongly discourage religious references and conversations altogether, ultimately creating an elephant in the room. This is known as a classic gray area wherein knowledge about policies and procedures are not fully disclosed.

Teacher and school staff training in how to incorporate religion into classroom lessons would make a meaningful workshop in public schools, but would public school principals consider it? If given the choice between offering teachers a workshop around religion or LGBTQIA issues, in today's climate, which might a school principal choose?

Even though knowing how to include religion into discussions and debates could add depth and improve the quality of learning, LGBTQIA is by far a more popular topic of choice for educational leaders. At the core of LGBTQIA is sexual preference, sexual feelings, sexual desire, and sexual confusion. Why would any school leader be more willing to address

LGBTQIA issues but ban religion altogether? What is the methodology for choosing what finds its way into a school district curriculum?

Everyone—school staff, principals, and students—can't help but bring their religious teachings, beliefs, and practices with them wherever they happen to be, even when entering a school building. Knowing the law and being provided training on what is permissible is a better approach to addressing legality concerning schools and religion. Otherwise, there is a gray area created wherein the reasons why religion is not permissible in schools is often not thoroughly explained to students, but is viewed by students as taboo. Then, religion has an unpleasant connotation attached to it.

## THE FORK IN THE ROAD

When choosing what remains in a curriculum and what goes, schools and parents should consider the benefits to children. Most importantly, schools and parents should consider how an addition can enhance the core subjects in a curriculum. For example, to find the proper balance regarding how religious discussions can unfold in schools, educators must first agree and make the case that prohibiting religious discussion altogether creates a learning deficit. Religion has historically prompted profound philosophical discussions in classrooms, creating a foundation for rigor to occur in the thinking process and in dialogues.

After all, when engaging in a debate, one uses every verbal weapon in his/her arsenal. Religion has long been one such resource from which many people have drawn wisdom, parallels, parables, and reasoning. These are all great elements that fold nicely into reading and writing. In terms of the years outlined in religious texts and how time was marked, those make for great lessons in mathematics.

Will any of us, irrespective of our religious backgrounds, ever come to an agreement when engaged in a debate about religion? That is not likely. Will today's generation ever understand the intellect it takes to agree to disagree? If you've ever engaged in a religious discussion, you know that it can be invigorating. Why? The individuals involved understand that they need to support their argument.

Because a religious argument can go on for an eternity, it is not always about winning the argument, but rather it is about supporting it to the best of one's ability. Allowing children to discuss elements that are pertinent to educational topics helps foster individuals who can argue from various perspectives, utilizing a variety of resources. Yet children, in many instances, are conditioned not to speak of religion in school. In large part, religion helped develop their moral fiber, can contribute greatly to school culture and climate, and can enhance classroom discussions and debates.

## CONCLUSION

Religion, which had long been a part of school culture, is becoming something of the distant past. However, not all religious elements have disappeared. If one were to review the shelves of many libraries in K-8 classrooms around the United States, one would likely find books on the Jewish culture, which is a religion, and literature on the persecution of Jews, which primarily was due to their religious beliefs; books on Muslims and their dress, religion, and culture would be prevalent; as well as books with pictures of Buddha; but one would be hard-pressed to find books on Christianity or books bearing pictures of the crucifix. Why? School and classroom libraries today strive to create cross-cultural pollination, but they often overlook the obvious.

For example, most people in the United States identify as Christian. Yet schools make the common mistake of oversight in securing sufficient Christian materials for libraries. In an effort to strike a cultural balance, schools assume that Christian children need to learn to appreciate other cultures besides their own. However, one has to begin with the study of self and see oneself reflected in classroom materials. Only then can an individual appreciate the cultural aspects of others—including other religions.

Often, when people are asked to name planets in the solar system, they will name all of the known planets except for their home planet, Earth. It may be somewhat instinctive to look beyond where you are because it appears more intriguing, but there is so much to be learned from the inside out. That is why it is important for schools to strike the right cultural and religious balance when selecting library materials that will appropriately reflect the beliefs of children of all religious backgrounds.

## Chapter Five

# Do Schools Contradict the Principles of Critical Thinking?

I didn't know I was a slave until I found out I couldn't do the things I wanted.
—Frederick Douglass

## WHAT DOES GRAY REPRESENT?

To be "in the pink" is a figure of speech that generally means to be in excellent health physically, mentally, and emotionally. In short, it means that all is well. In education, there is an appearance of intellectual soundness as it relates to the acceptance of others' lifestyles and cultural differences. However, one can have the façade of being intelligent in certain areas of life, but at the same time, lack the necessary depth to think through a variety of issues, topics, and situations, and thus, end up in a gray area.

There are many aspects to cultural and lifestyle awareness that directly correlate with critical thinking. Presently there is a push to get children to have a total acceptance of all people, with their cultures, lifestyles, and numerous other differences. This is a noble idea and one worth pursuing in societies, but how we, in education, approach this goal is of upmost importance.

In America today, there are far more ethnic groups represented than there were just thirty years ago, and the percentages are projected to significantly increase. According to the Pew Research Center (Cohn & Caumont, 2016), "By 2055, the U.S. will not have a single racial or ethnic majority." Much of this change has been (and will be) driven by immigration, which will be discussed more in depth later in this book (see chapter 8).

According to current social norms, the ideal scenario is to encourage children to blend—to tolerate and accept cultural differences. In addition to schools teaching the acceptance of cultural differences, there is also the lifestyle choice element—lesbian, gay, bisexual, transgender, questioning/queer, intersex, and asexual (LGBTQIA). As groups of people from varied backgrounds accept one another's cultures and lifestyle choices, there are layers and nuances associated with the process of unification that are complex.

Quite frankly, schools don't have the time to dedicate to properly develop a rich understanding of all the different cultures and lifestyles that blend together in a given country. Because there is little time to spend truly developing the art of appreciating cultures and lifestyle choices during the school day, most schools adopt a quick-fix approach—acceptance of all, without question, simply based on the fact that people exist.

In a process such as this, there is little thinking involved. Instead, this method of teaching children to appreciate lifestyle and cultural differences is more akin to conditioning. Thus, children have the appearance of being "in the pink." But rather, emotionally and intellectually, they are actually in a gray area.

## NATURAL REACTIONS TO GRAY

After people have been in a gray zone for a long period of time, inevitably the fog lifts and the process of questioning begins. It is human curiosity that leads a person to seek clarity and truth for oneself, and this often leads to pushback against "truths" that have been imposed. A good historical example of this is the Boston Tea Party.

The Boston Tea Party was symbolic of many things that are inherent in a free world—freedom of expression being one. The primary motivation of this act was England's increase in the tea tax. That was the tipping point. The act of dumping tea into the ocean clearly demonstrated the strong desire of the people of the new land to stand on principle, govern their own thinking, and be independent. These individuals set their destiny on a new course. That is the inheritance of today's society. How one maximizes an inheritance is quite another thing.

In the famous 1960 movie *Inherit the Wind*—about a teacher on trial for teaching Darwin's theory of evolution, a story loosely based on the Scopes Trial of 1925—while being cross-examined by the lawyer, played by Spencer Tracey, the reverend replied, "I do not think about things that I do not think about." Not only was this a humorous line, but it was an interesting one, because it was indicative of an individual who had landed in a gray area.

Is there fear in present-day society that if people are left to do their "own thinking" regarding culture and lifestyle, they may draw the "wrong" conclusions? Then the question becomes: What is the "right" conclusion—especially in a country like the United States, which still recognizes the first amendment of the constitution protecting freedom of speech? Coupled with freedom of speech is the freedom to discern for oneself.

The proper translation of freedom of speech is freedom of thought, as there cannot be a discourse without first having consideration. Those who come to know the richness of other cultures are usually touched by those cultures in a variety of ways, and will often incorporate positive attributes of other cultures into their own lives. This is when true intelligence is demonstrated. By experiencing other cultures firsthand and through reading about other lands and ethnicities, one makes one's own human connections to those experiences.

When an individual arrives at a conclusion on his or her own, there are associations made and an intellect that is exercised, which cannot be duplicated by simple cues. Taking a Marxist approach to the cultural acceptance of individual differences is not a viable means for building real aptitude in children to bridge cultural relationships and foster an understanding of different lifestyles. Because each individual is obviously unique, their acceptance of something or someone is, therefore, reached at a respective time frame.

Each person's makeup is markedly different. A form of intelligence is demonstrated when we come to appreciate differences in one another of our own accord, not simply because someone told us to do so. A better approach to appreciating cultural differences is to expose children to culture in different forms and then allow them to draw their own conclusions.

This is where schools can make a difference. For example, educators have flexibility in how they group children for school projects, arrange children in reading groups, couple children for field trips, line up a variety of speakers to address the class, and allow children to share cultural experiences that align with classroom lessons.

Families have a greater reach with regard to exposing children to different cultures and ethnicities than do schools. There are venues that are amenable to families for introducing young minds to culture, such as art museums, family outings (in a variety of neighborhoods), inviting diverse children to birthday parties or play dates, and coordinating family movie outings that explore a range of cultural variances—followed by family discussions. These provide more natural ways for children to interact with assorted types of individuals and experience different cultures and lifestyles with the opportunity to have more in-depth discussions with their families at home.

Postman (1996) wrote,

> A museum is, in a fundamental sense, a political institution. For its answers to the question, "what does it mean to be a human being?" must be given within the context of a specific moment in history and must inevitably be addressed to living people who, as always, are struggling with the problems of moral, psychological, and social survival. . . . A museum, after all, tells a story. And like the oral and written literature of any culture, its story may serve to awaken the better angels of our nature or to stimulate what is fiendish. (165).

Here Postman refers to the benefits of exposing individuals to knowledge about aspects of various cultures, and the freedom of choice to accept or reject that knowledge. It is the natural course of learning.

Change often entails compromise. Therefore, change should not be a haphazard process. It seems that in education, where sleight of hand can have lasting negative effects on children's futures, society would seek out a more effective method of socializing children.

## The Ever-Present Issues for School Districts to Consider in Education

- Which items should be introduced into a curriculum?
- Which items should school districts consider bringing back into a curriculum?
- Which items have no place in a school curriculum?

## LESBIAN, GAY, BISEXUAL, TRANSGENDER, QUESTIONING, INTERSEX, ASEXUAL (LGBTQIA)

When changes emerge, something will likely be lost. It becomes a matter of what a system is willing to trade. Most children in the United States, by the time they are fourteen years old, know that the unwritten protocol for navigating their adolescent years is to appear to be pro–lesbian, gay, transgender, bisexual, questioning, intersex, and asexual (LGBTQIA), whether or not they themselves practice the lifestyle, agree, or disagree with it. Conversely, most children understand that to speak about their religion in U.S. schools is frowned upon. (This will be addressed in the next chapter of this book.)

While schools are often on pins and needles about how and when to allow religious utterance or discussion in the classroom, many are trying to find ways to introduce LGBTQIA elements into school curricula. It is a topic that arises frequently during education conferences.

Are young children being indoctrinated into the gay lifestyle? According to *Merriam-Webster's Dictionary*, the word *indoctrinate* means "to instruct especially in fundamentals or rudiments." By introducing LGBTQIA to elementary- and middle-school-age children, it introduces a homosexual lifestyle to them at an early age. Even if the lessons on LGBTQIA don't explicitly teach about homosexuality, the seed is planted. This indoctrination not only materializes in some schools, but also in news sources, books, films made for children, and online sources.

As schools around the United States are contemplating whether or not to infuse components of LGBTQIA lessons into school curricula, they must consider that there are limited hours per day in the classroom. Properly teaching children the intricate issues surrounding LGBTQIA requires time. And because the heart of LGBTQIA deals with sex and sexuality, is it even appropriate to introduce the subject to the lower grade levels?

That question is valid, because ultimately children will question the difference between a heterosexual relationship and a homosexual relationship. Children will wonder, as only kids can, what is at the heart of the differences between the two. It becomes a question of: Is teaching kids about LGBTQIA so important to their learning that we are willing to trade their innocence to include it in a curriculum?

And why should adults introduce homosexuality to young children in the first place? What is the advantage? Currently, what is the trade-off for children who are already conditioned to respond in the affirmative to LGBTQIA topics?

These are questions at the top of mind for those who oppose the introduction of LGBTQIA topics in elementary and middle schools. For example, parents in San Ramon, California, petitioned against a proposed LBTGQ acceptance week. In an article featured on the ABC7 website (2016), in referring to parents, the author wrote, "They created an online petition asking that it only be a day, not a week. They're concerned this will indoctrinate children and humiliate those whose religions don't agree with the campaigns."

Not only are parents concerned about school curriculums, but they are also concerned about LGBTQIA intimacy in children's movies. For example, the *Atlantic* (Nikolas, 2014) published an article entitled "It's Not Just *Frozen*: Most Disney Movies Are Pro-Gay." In 2014, there were those who viewed this type of generalization as an overexaggeration.

However, fast-forward to the year 2017 and Disney's introduction of the first gay kiss to its young viewing audience in the movie *Beauty and the Beast* (*USA Today*, 2017). One drive-in theater in Alabama canceled the screening of the updated version of *Beauty and the Beast*, posting on its Facebook page, "When companies continually force their views on us, we need to take a stand."

The downside is that most children don't fully understand the scope of LGBTQIA, yet there is an almost automatic acceptance that is currently reinforced by schools, media, and society. On the other hand, many children are urged to say no to classroom discussions around religion, which is a cultural aspect deeply engrained in most children's family values, and one that helps them maintain their innocence.

Mastery of critical thinking takes time to scaffold, and children typically arrive at that place through problem-solving, decision-making, and parent and teacher facilitation of those processes. However, critical thinking cannot be mastered through the memorization of rote, blanket responses to certain issues and topics. Have children in today's society landed in a gray area in this regard?

Any civilized society strives for a nation in which people of varied backgrounds can peacefully coexist. There have been many examples of human struggle in the form of civil movements, and sometimes even war, as it relates to integrating ethnic backgrounds, cultural backgrounds, and lifestyles in an effort to enhance the quality of life for all who coexist in an eclectic society. The saying, "Rome wasn't built in a day" remains relevant. Subsequently, children cannot be expected to form intelligent opinions about others at a rapid pace. Yet that is the expectation.

In our attempt to create societies of "enlightened" children who are completely accepting of others, there is a fine line between free-range thinking and conditioning. The *Funk and Wagnall Dictionary* defines a *conditioned response* as a "learned response to a previously neutral stimulus, made directly effective with its repeated association with a stimulus normally evoking the response." According to this definition, both *LGBTQIA* and *religion*, although evoking very different responses, are the stimulus in schools today.

Conditioning in education can be masked with phrases like, "That's not appropriate," or "You shouldn't say that," in response to a child's honest feelings about a particular topic, circumstance, or person. This summation excludes derogatory or hurtful statements made by children that are directed toward others. However, when children utter simple honest inquires regarding people and situations, they are often reprimanded, even if their utterances are mere questions that stem from natural curiosity.

The best question any of us can ask a child is: What prompted that statement? Too often, adults do not ask that simple, but poignant question. This is where caution in how we proceed in education is warranted, especially as it concerns how children form opinions.

## THE GOVERNMENT'S ROLE

If schools are to strike a balance, then the right type of training has to be funded and administered to school staff. Also, the big question is: What's necessary and appropriate for young minds? In some cases, politicians are relentless when it comes to winning votes and will burden schools financially on a whim.

For example, in 2016, as the U.S. presidential election was fast approaching, President Obama focused his attention on a North Carolina law known as House Bill 2 (HB2), which reads: "Transgender people who have not taken surgical and legal steps to change the gender noted on their birth certificate have no legal right to use public restrooms of the gender which they identify."

In a swift reaction to this state law, and perhaps to gain favor for the Democratic Party as the election approached, and in particular from gay voters, President Obama quickly took a position on this topic, and as a result a letter was generated by the federal government and sent to school districts. The letter was specific to schools and their transgender population of students, of which the majority of schools had none.

The online version of *Time* magazine (2016) stated: "The Obama Administration wrote every public-school district in the country Friday warning local administrators they have to let transgender students use bathrooms matching their gender identity." The article went on to state, "The guidance signed by Justice and Education officials, while not a legal decree, implicitly threatens noncompliant schools with lawsuits or the withdrawal of federal funding." The letter can be found in full at the end of this chapter. (See item 1B.)

Transgender students in America make up such a small population that the focus it garnered at the level of the federal government was viewed by many as sheer sensationalism. It left many people asking: Why is the president of the United States focused on such a non-urgent issue like transgender bathroom options for students, when there are so many other major areas of concern in education that impact far more young people?

There are a plethora of immediate concerns that affect a larger number of children directly that could be infused into a school district's curriculum and facilitated by presidential focus and support, including signs and warnings of mental health issues among youth and how to seek related help, navigating the financial aspects of college and career (which many families struggle with), and addressing the various drug epidemics in the United States. These are just a few major concerns that could take precedence over the focus on sexuality.

LGBTQIA has become a hot topic at education conferences around the globe. There is a rush in societies to find an immediate result to the "hot topic of the day," for which there is no neat, one-and-done solution. According to the *Washington Post* (Somashekhar, 2014), the 2014 Center for Disease Control Survey demonstrates that the percentage of those who consider themselves gay, lesbian, or bisexual in the United States totals 1.6 percent of adults.

Surveys in the United States vary and have been quoted as high as 3.5 percent. The number of children who identify as gay or transgender are obscure at best. Even the famed *New York Times* was hard-pressed to state an exact number of children who identify as transgender: Its Health Section headline (Hoffman, 2016) read "As Attention Grows, Transgender Children's Numbers Are Elusive."

That stated, there are students around the country with concrete test scores that are below the norm in reading, writing, and mathematics. For example, according to the news outlet ABC13.com (2014), more than forty Houston schools were considered to be "failing." The article stated, "It's not a good report card statewide. The number of failing schools, according to the TEA, has almost doubled in the last year."

In 2016, Texas test scores would again be in the news. The *Texas Tribune* (Collier, 2016) reported, "Last year 55 school districts and charters—or 4.5 percent—were in the failing, or 'improvement required' category; this year, it's 66, or 5.5 percent."

In that same year, 2016, the New York State Department released a document stating that 188 schools had been identified as Priority Schools. Schools earned this title when they were among the lowest-scoring schools in the state, had not demonstrated progress in math and English language arts, or had persistently low graduation rates. There would be no emergency document drafted by the U.S. Department of Justice and the U.S. Department of Education to be sent to school districts where low test scores were consistent. No, the public school system would not be receiving the urgent type of attention it needed regarding academic success for all children.

Yet both the U.S. Department of Justice and the U.S. Department of Education chose to direct the public's attention toward a transgender bathroom issue that was not a widespread concern. (See the original letter sent to states, figure 1.2.) Have schools become a political football? As if schools didn't have enough to accomplish, they inadvertently were being asked to consider building or finding some other means of making concessions for a transgender population of students—*that didn't even exist* in most schools!

Is there a danger of transgender children being bullied? Yes. But any child can be a target of bullying for various reasons. Schools get a better return on their efforts when they strengthen their core—improving teaching and learning in basic subject areas, retaining knowledgeable leadership and teachers, and aligning efforts with parents in myriad ways—not just through PTAs.

Newspaper headlines and politicians who want to elicit votes from particular groups cannot continue to drive these erratic changes in schools. Change should be based on need. Who better to conduct a needs assessment of students, free of politics, than those who live in the communities and work in the school districts?

In recent years, educators have complained of the looming feeling that they are under siege. This is largely contributed to the increasing financial gain of those who drive initiatives in education, ranging from the media to entrepreneurs. With so many changes coming down the pike, initiated by individuals who do not have intricate knowledge about the feasibility of proposed educational changes, teachers and principals juggle a stream of initiatives that they don't have time to fully examine. This applies to initiatives that are being tossed out or are being incorporated into curricula.

## THE IMPORTANCE OF DEFINING "NORMAL"

"Normal" is a gauge by which we all live. Children have always looked to the adults in their lives to establish a basis for "normal." There is a normal range for everything in life, from the pH balance of the human body to the norms that are established for academic testing. Humans are biologically created, and thus there are scientific norms for humans, as well. Why is establishing a norm for children so important?

In sports, there are those who adhere to the theory that all children are winners. However, does that prepare children for a realistic world? In a CNN article (Jones, 2015), which discussed whether or not children deserved a participation trophy, the writer, Roxanne Jones, had the following to say: "I get it. It may be more comfortable to tell our children that 'trying your best is all that matters,' but we adults know this to be a lie. How exactly does this lie best prepare our children for the harsh realities of life?" Jones's statement could be compared with other confusing mixed messages we send children. Children look to adults to help them gauge what is normal. Parents cannot leave this task to the media.

Today, even parents feel some pressure to avoid making unpopular statements at PTA meetings, for fear that their child might be viewed as "different," and there exists an even greater fear that their child might be treated differently by staff and peers in school as they move forward. When parents feel the pressure to respond in alignment with popular thought, they then set a standard for what children will frame as "normal," even though that is not the parent's intent.

For example, increasingly, children who question the lifestyle of the LGBTQIA community, in today's society, are mocked or viewed as dim-witted. This is a very different scenario from the prevalent attitudes in the

1950s, 1960s, and 1970s, when the LGBTQIA community was striving to be openly accepted by society.

While doing so, many in the LGBTQIA community were ridiculed themselves, and some were even physically attacked for expressing their homosexual preferences. However, they found strength in voicing their opinions—something that kids today are deterred from doing in school. Countless numbers of children today question LGBTQIA partnerships, for they come from homes that have traditional mother-and-father alliances. For many, that is their norm.

Even if their parents are separated or divorced, having parents who represent the male and female sexes is still how the majority of children are raised in the United States today. Therefore, that is the norm to which most children have become accustomed. However, when these children have natural, innocent questions concerning the lifestyle of the LGBTQIA community, they are often met with comments by teachers like, "Well, everyone has the right to be who they are." This is undoubtedly a true statement.

However, if you are a child, then the way you perceive such a statement is that this topic is off-limits—not only to in-depth discussion, but to any dialogue at all. In fact, most schools are afraid to go in-depth about LGBTQIA for fear of liability. So, why entertain a topic that cannot be fully comprehended by a young mind? In addition, schools are not equipped to fully explore, or fully fund such a project. These two concerns alone place schools in a gray area here.

Was this the intention of LGBTQIA groups when the idea of educating children about the LGBTQIA community arose? Many in the LGBTQIA community were themselves, silenced at one time. There is a reverse discrimination taking shape now, however, that has the potential to polarize people in our society. There is a conditioning that often takes place around issues of acceptance rather than providing a real education to children about what it means to exist systemically in a society—with everyone. That is a more intelligent approach than simply expecting people to fall in line with individual lifestyle choices, cultures, and ideologies without debate or discussion.

Since the early 1990s, school districts have been grappling with whether or not to include lessons about the gay lifestyle into curricula across the United States. The other debate has been at what age those lessons should begin. Meanwhile, parents in force have steadily protested the inclusion of LGBTQIA in most school curriculums. Parents who have fought against LGBTQIA elements being infused into curriculums have done so primarily because they do not want their children to view the LGBTQIA lifestyle as "normal."

There have been decades of discussions regarding this issue. Over two decades ago, a *New York Times* article (Celis, 1993) captured the tone of the first real attempts at implementing LGBTQIA in schools across the United States. The *New York Times* writer William Celis III once stated, "New York City's angry debate over including lessons about gay and lesbian families in the public curriculum has overshadowed a growing movement nationwide: Many of the largest school districts are quietly and cautiously adding such lessons to their curriculums."

He went on to detail how some school districts were introducing the topic to children: "New York City has taken the most aggressive stance among any school system by asking teachers to mention alternative families and life styles in the curriculum as early as the first grade. . . . For secondary school students, lessons tend to be more directly about homosexuality. . . . In Fairfax County, VA., Public Schools, high school students view a 29-minute film, 'What If I'm Gay?' In other cases, school districts seek local gay and lesbian groups to talk to students about homosexuality." The article went on to state that "from the seventh grade on, San Francisco public school students are taught formal lessons about same-sex families and about homosexuality, including presentations from gay and lesbian groups."

In 2015, according to the *Washington Post*, "The Fairfax County School Board has approved expanding the school system's sex education curriculum to include teaching teenagers in grades 7–10 about gender identity and transgender issues."

Who stands to benefit from the implementation of introducing LGBTQIA in schools? The introduction of LGBTQIA can, again, be a huge benefit to companies that produce and sell related materials as well as those who are shareholders in such companies. Schools have a way of taking new ideas and implementing elements of those concepts prematurely—not fully understanding the intentions or the most effective way to unfold initiatives. In addition, schools do not have the time to thoroughly educate children on a topic such as this. Therefore, schools have to be cautious in what they agree to undertake, as children are at their most impressionable stages in life while under their care and guidance.

Does the study of LGBTQIA issues create more confusion than clarity for children? In recent years, children in the United States have grown up watching our nation's leaders flip-flop on LGBTQIA issues, leaving children short of public figures who are willing to stand by a decision, even when it is not a popular one. All adults can look back on how they were raised, and most of us were anchored in some belief system.

What will be the anchor for children of today? It might be wise for children to begin their lives with some strong beliefs—something to provide direction and a sense of purpose. Switching fundamental beliefs with no real basis for doing so, simply because it is the "popular" thing to do, is not a stable foundation for anyone, particularly children. And with a bombardment of LGBTQIA issues in their lives, many children would probably define "normal" as "I don't know." That is a recipe for a real identity crisis.

**1B**

**U.S. Departments of Education and Justice Release Joint Guidance to Help Schools Ensure the Civil Rights of Transgender Students**

May 13, 2016

Contact: Press Office, (202) 401-1576, press@ed.gov

The U.S. Departments of Education and Justice released joint guidance today to help provide educators the information they need to ensure that all students, including transgender students, can attend school in an environment free from discrimination based on sex.

Recently, questions have arisen from school districts, colleges and universities, and others about transgender students and how to best ensure these students, and non-transgender students, can all enjoy a safe and discrimination-free environment.

Under Title IX of the Education Amendments of 1972, schools receiving federal money may not discriminate based on a student's sex, including a student's transgender status. The guidance makes clear that both federal agencies treat a student's gender identity as the student's sex for purposes of enforcing Title IX.

"No student should ever have to go through the experience of feeling unwelcome at school or on a college campus," said U.S. Secretary of Education John B. King Jr. "This guidance further clarifies what we've said repeatedly—that gender identity is protected under Title IX. Educators want to do the right thing for students, and many have reached out to us for guidance on how to follow the law. We must ensure that our young people know that whoever they are or wherever they come from, they have the opportunity to get a great education in an environment free from discrimination, harassment and violence."

"There is no room in our schools for discrimination of any kind, including discrimination against transgender students on the basis of their sex," said Attorney General Loretta E. Lynch. "This guidance gives administrators, teachers, and parents the tools they need to protect transgender students from peer harassment and to identify and address unjust school policies. I look forward to continuing our work with the Department of Education—and with schools across the country—to create classroom environments that are safe, nurturing, and inclusive for all of our young people."

"Our federal civil rights law guarantees all students, including transgender students, the opportunity to participate equally in school programs and activities without sex discrimination as a core civil right," said Department of Education Assistant Secretary for Civil Rights Catherine E. Lhamon. "This guidance answers questions schools have been asking, with a goal to ensure that all students are treated equally consistent with their gender identity. We look forward to continuing to work with schools and school communities to satisfy Congress' promise of equality for all."

"Every child deserves to attend school in a safe, supportive environment that allows them to thrive and grow. And we know that teachers and administrators care deeply about all of their students and want them to succeed in school and life," said Principal Deputy Assistant Attorney General Vanita Gupta, head of the Justice Department's Civil Rights Division. "Our guidance sends a clear message to transgender students across the country: here in America, you are safe, you are protected and you belong—just as you are. We look forward to working with school officials to make the promise of equal opportunity a reality for all of our children."

The guidance explains that when students or their parents, as appropriate, notify a school that a student is transgender, the school must treat the student consistent with the student's gender identity. A school may not require transgender students to have a medical diagnosis, undergo any medical treatment, or produce a birth certificate or other identification document before treating them consistent with their gender identity.

The guidance also explains schools' obligations to:

- Respond promptly and effectively to sex-based harassment of all students, including harassment based on a student's actual or perceived gender identity, transgender status, or gender transition;
- Treat students consistent with their gender identity even if their school records or identification documents indicate a different sex;
- Allow students to participate in sex-segregated activities and access sex-segregated facilities consistent with their gender identity; and
- Protect students' privacy related to their transgender status under Title IX and the Family Educational Rights and Privacy Act.

At the same time, the guidance makes clear that schools can provide additional privacy options to any student for any reason. The guidance does not require any student to use shared bathrooms or changing spaces, when, for example, there are other appropriate options available; and schools can also take steps to increase privacy within shared facilities.

In addition to the Departments' joint Title IX guidance, the Department of Education's Office of Elementary and Secondary Education also released Examples of Policies and Emerging Practices for Supporting Transgender Students, a compilation of policies and practices that schools across the country are already using to support transgender students. The document shares some common questions on topics such as school records, privacy, and terminology, and then explains how some state and school district policies have answered these questions, which may be useful for other states and school districts that are considering these issues. In this document, the Education Department does not endorse any particular policy, but offers examples from actual policies to help educators develop policies and practices for their own schools.

Many parents, schools, and districts have raised questions about this area of civil rights law. Together, these documents will help navigate what may be a new terrain for some.

The mission of ED's Office for Civil Rights (OCR) is to ensure equal access to education and promote educational excellence throughout the nation through the vigorous enforcement of civil rights. OCR is responsible for enforcing federal civil rights laws that prohibit discrimination by educational institutions on the basis of race, color, national origin, disability, sex and age, as well as the Boy Scouts of America Equal Access Act of 2001. Additional information about OCR is available here.

The mission of ED's Office of Elementary and Secondary Education (OESE) is to promote academic excellence, enhance educational opportunities and equity for all of America's children and families, and to improve the quality of teaching and learning by providing leadership, technical assistance, and financial support. Additional information about OESE is available here.

The Department of Justice's Civil Rights Division, created in 1957 by the enactment of the Civil Rights Act of 1957, works to uphold the civil and constitutional rights of all Americans, particularly some of the most vulnerable members of our society. The division enforces federal statutes prohibiting discrimination on the basis of race, color, sex, disability, religion, familial status and national origin. Additional information about the Civil Rights Division of the Justice Department is available here.

## Chapter Six

# Kids Will Be Kids

Children must be taught how to think, not what to think. —Margaret Mead

## LGBTQIA — WHAT'S ALL THE FUSS ABOUT?

The lesbian, gay, bisexual, transgender, queer/questioning, intersex, and asexual (LGBTQIA) lifestyle is sometimes considered one that is chosen by those who are a part of that community. Some research suggests that there may be a biological component to this choice, but most research is inconclusive. The *Los Angeles Times* (Healy, 2015) reported: "Could the molecular signals that turn genes on and off reveal a person's sexual orientation? New research identifies epigenomic 'marks' linked to homosexuality. But experts say the origins of partner preference remain a mystery, and that the research is insufficient."

The *Washington Times* (Richardson, 2016) quoted Dr. Mayer, a biostatistician and epidemiologist trained in psychology, as saying, "I'm not suggesting the statement [that gay and transgender people are 'born that way'] is false." Dr. Mayer went on to state: "I'm saying there isn't enough scientific evidence to support the statement."

There has been very little recent research to discover whether or not gay people are biologically different from heterosexuals, and whether parents and educators are prematurely looking at children differently as they try to discover whether a child has gay tendencies or is a possible transgender individual. Is this a relevant topic for K–8 schools?

Kids are naturally creative. Many adults lived through fantasy youths, pretending to be various characters, inventing stories, and even inventing new identities. Ironically, some adults wish they could have retained their imaginative capabilities from childhood, as that is always useful when trying to tap in to creative thought.

Over the years, young girls have sung along to hit songs by male vocalists. Similarly, some young boys have been enthralled with female singers like Cher or Aretha Franklin. Just a few decades ago, this was viewed as normal behavior. There were tomboyish girls in every neighborhood, and some boys were not as athletic as others.

Not every child looks the same or behaves the same. A child's creativity is demonstrated in many facets of their lives—not just in the learning process. From an educational perspective, kids are imaginative.

Throughout time, teenagers have always tried out new fads. For girls, sometimes it was donning a male's oversized shirt with shorts or jeans, or sporting a man's hat for the sake of fashion. At one time, a "man bag" was popular for teen boys, and some even idolized singers such as Boy George. Did it mean that these particular young people were leaning toward a transgender lifestyle? Not necessarily. It is more likely that they were simply exploring the social landscape around them, experimenting with the look, sound, and feel of things—all a natural part of learning. In the not-too-distant past, young people had the opportunity to discover who they were and the world around them without the threat of being labeled. Nowadays, those labels go well beyond words.

Parents and school officials now seek to discover if a child is possibly transgender. If parents suspect that a child is "transgender," they may start that child on a puberty blocker at the beginning of a child's puberty. This process is primarily designed for children who believe they belong in the body of the opposite sex. A PBS *Frontline* report (2015) noted, "What makes treatment tricky is that there is no test that can tell whether a child experiencing stress about their gender will grow up to be transgender."

The report went on to state, "The benefit of the blockers is that they block hormone-induced biological changes, such as vocal cord changes, the development of breast tissue or changes in facial structure." There are a lot of natural changes that a child who undergoes treatment will miss. In labeling children, educators and parents need to consider the seeds that this type of classification can plant in the mind of a child.

Doctors are not sure of the long-term effects that suppressing puberty will have on children, as this is a new approach to dealing with children suspected of being transgender. But why is society even seeking to transition children at such an early age—as early as nine years old, which is when puberty can start for some children? (PBS *Frontline*, 2015). Shouldn't children be allowed to first navigate their rocky adolescent years before a decision is made about their gender treatment?

Does the labeling that occurs today add another layer of gray to kids' paths as they head toward adulthood—college and career? If left to their own natural "growing pains" without adults trying to "fix" every facet of their lives, would they not figure out their own directions as young adults, just as previous generations did before them?

Are educators and parents overthinking and overanalyzing natural child behaviors? These days, every movement of a child is scrutinized through the lens of gender. Often, this topic overshadows even the academic needs of students. In particular, many parents and school officials are buying in to the transgender campaign that is taking shape in the media and in politics.

According to psychologist Ken Zucker in an interview with NPR (2008), when asked how many children he typically sees, he stated: "Usually we see one new [gender identity disorder] child a week, maybe more. One of the interesting developments is an increase in referrals. Before we had fifteen or twenty kids on the waiting list. Now we have eighty-eight."

In the last decade, kids have been on the superhighway of media exposure. Is it possible that some young children, who are professing to be trapped in the wrong body, are doing so simply because they have seen other children in media outlets claiming to be transgender?

During the NPR interview (Spiegel, 2008), Dr. Zucker further stated, "There are so many kids we see in the clinic where the desire to change their sex goes away, for whatever reason. So, there are many kids we'd see in adolescence and you'd never have known gender identity was an issue for them in childhood." Simply put, kids love attention. Are parents and educators jumping the gun when it comes to identifying and labeling kids as potential transgender individuals?

## CONFUSION IN THE LEARNING ENVIRONMENT

In this "fast-food"—or "microwave"—society, many rush to find swift solutions. The fact is, life is messy. Yes, for various reasons, life is confusing and painful for most young people during their adolescent years. However, childhood will run its course. The heavy focus on LGBTQIA in education and in the media, however, could likely cause more confusion than clarity for children.

Many within the LGBTQIA community probably fell into the Q (questioning category) for a period of time before declaring themselves one of the other LGBTQIA types. Yet, in schools, children are expected to accept the complex LGBTQIA lifestyle without question. There is a huge push in schools for the acceptance of certain elements of sexuality without the necessary mental maturity to understand such a topic.

In many ways, sexuality determines the direction of one's life. For a wide range of children, their religion expresses different viewpoints about LGBTQIA. Yet, religious discussion is not embraced in many classrooms across the United States. Is it fair, then, to inject one without the other? This can be very confusing for children, as this leaves only a narrow space for moral arguments from young minds about a variety of issues surrounding LGBTQIA. Children are simply expected to accept a lifestyle they cannot fully comprehend. So, why even introduce it in schools?

Effective, purposeful LGBTQIA implementation in schools will be next to impossible to roll out, primarily due to several factors: time constraints within a given school day, solid justification for implementation over other pressing issues, the fact that most educators don't fully understand LGBTQIA themselves, and the lack of proper funding to prepare teachers on how to effectively navigate the topic.

The *New York Times* (Davis, 2017) published an article about a parent whose child was labeled a tomboy by her friends. The parent of the student stated, "When kids say she's in the wrong bathroom, she tells them, 'I'm a girl,' and invariably they say, 'Oh, ok.'" The article continued discussing a child's innocent response to this type of situation versus an adult's response. The parent went on to explain, "The kids get it. But the grown-ups do not. While celebrating the diversity of sexual and gender identities, we also need to celebrate tomboys and other girls who fall outside the narrow confines to gender roles. Don't tell them that they're not girls."

She continued, "Yet she is asked by the pediatrician, by her teachers, by people who have known her for many years, if she feels like, or wants to be called, or wants to be, a boy . . . when they continue to question her gender identity—and are skeptical of her response—the message they send is that a girl cannot look and act like her and still be a girl."

## CAUTION IN PREMATURE LABELING OF KIDS

What happens when kids are mislabeled? In terms of the recent attention around transgender youth, why risk emotional damage to a child that could be irreversible? From a teaching perspective, if there is a possibility that a child is simply going through a phase and parents fan the flames, this could cause a disruption in the teaching and learning process.

Kids need to show up to school in an optimal frame of mind. But jumping the gun, and adding another layer of what could amount to emotional turmoil in a child's life, could grossly affect their ability to focus on their studies. For parents who are considering puberty-blocker treatment for their pubescent child, one question to consider is: Who stands to profit?

Puberty blockers open up a new financial market for profiteers. Psychiatry, hospitals, pharmaceutical companies, and those who invest in these entities stand to gain a great deal. A little caution in how the adults in a child's life proceed in this area could go a long way toward creating healthy, happy young adults. When children reach adulthood, they will have plenty of time to make their own life choices. Schools can help students focus on a good educational foundation, so that when they become adults, they can make better, informed choices about their lives.

How well thought out are inclusions and exclusions in school curricula? Many changes in recent decades seem to have been knee-jerk reactions. After all, there are only so many hours in the school day in which to prepare young intellects for life's challenges. The topic of LGBTQIA is pretty much open and shut. It does not seem to carry with it all the usual great ingredients that can realistically be unpacked in a K–8 classroom.

Let's face it, the LGBTQIA community took a stance and stood by their decision to go against the standard, attempting to redefine societal norms. But shouldn't children be afforded the same opportunity—to say, "I agree" or "I disagree" with certain aspects of any lifestyle? And let's not forget the phrase, "And here is my argument." It is wise to make room for such statements during classroom lessons, but there is not time for such lengthy arguments during a class session. If teachers are required to incorporate LGBTQIA elements into the school day, one can be sure that the teachers' goals will be met, even if the topic cannot fully be debated or explored by students. That's the reality.

## CONCLUSION

With so many changes in education streaming top down, many teachers are overwhelmed and seem to be teaching on autopilot, which is a dangerous zone for any educator. School leaders and teachers are so focused on trying to figure out how to implement one change before another is manufactured at the government level, and school districts blindly implement practices out of fear of retaliation by the federal and state governments. There is always the looming threat of government officials withholding funds from school districts when they are not in compliance. That compliance can apply to any number of areas—from classroom lessons to leaky roofs in school buildings.

Often, teaching skills for new implementations have not yet been mastered by educators before the federal government has alerted states that yet another new initiative is in the works. This leaves educators little time to ask: How and why are certain topics selected to be introduced to children in classrooms? In many cases, teachers and school leaders simply roll out the initiatives to avoid any punitive reactions from the state and federal governments.

Will generations to come enjoy the freedom of standing firm on their beliefs, even if that sometimes means standing alone? In our quest in education to close learning gaps between the United States and other countries like China, India, and Finland, the United States would be careless to abandon its primary strength—freedom of expression.

"We can agree to disagree" is a catchphrase that is slowly disappearing. If Western culture continues along this vein, many children will not ever know the beauty and the art of that concept. The LGBTQIA community has stood up for what it believes in, and in some cases, many of these individuals stood up for what they viewed as their right to be different in the face of their families, communities, and workplaces.

Some of those in the gay community are not in favor of the way in which young children are now being inundated with elements of the LGBTQIA lifestyle. Regarding the gay kiss in the movie *Beauty and the Beast*, Joseph Murray II, an openly gay lawyer in Mississippi, had this to say: "Somewhere along the line, Disney went off course. No longer did it see itself as a defender of children's innocence." He went on to say, "Why do we have to expose our kids to such mature themes? Do they not have plenty of time to grow up? Or maybe the point is to make them grow up too soon, and that is where I part ways with my community" (*Orlando Sentinel*, 2017).

Could it be that, in education, we are trying to do the right thing by teaching tolerance and acceptance, but we are getting it wrong in how we are doing it? There is a lesson to be learned from the LGBTQIA community about agreeing to disagree, but still maintaining mutual respect for one another as individuals. In today's society, children seem fearful of being perceived as different regarding hot button topics such as religion and LGBTQIA.

Remaining silent about important issues does not translate to enlightenment or enhance creativity, and it does not promote critical thinking in education. There is a sense that the government is bullying schools into agreeing with these new changes in education, regardless of whether those changes reflect the needs of a particular community. This is a direct threat to community control and local choice.

Chapters 5 and 6 of this book are not an anti-LGTBQIA dissertation. Instead, these chapters question how politicians and school boards choose which topics to include in curricula and which to carve out. They also outline the quick-solution approaches to teaching children about inclusiveness, which is a very involved process.

In the next chapter, this book will look at an intelligent approach for getting kids to appreciate people who are different from themselves—everything from a person's cultural background to a person's skill sets. Critical thinking involves making connections on one's own. If children can see the connectivity of man, and the links between, and everything else, then perhaps there will be less need for schools and society to use ill-considered solutions for getting kids to be accepting and tolerant of others.

## Chapter Seven

# Lessons in Systems Thinking

Our Scientific Power has outrun our spiritual power. We have guided missiles and misguided men. —Dr. Martin Luther King Jr.

## TEACHING CHILDREN ABOUT SYSTEMS THINKING

There is a balance to navigating life. Parents and educators can help children achieve a sense of balance as it relates to their studies, emotional growth, and cultural awareness. Systems thinking can help in the development of children in all three areas. It only needs to be introduced to children and shown how to apply it to all aspects of life. In this chapter, we will further examine specific ways to apply systems thinking.

Johnson (2004) stated in *The Queen of Education*: "I expect my students to be responsible for their behavior, and I do not allow them to make me or anybody else responsible." There is a certain responsibility that goes along with being a part of society. Regardless of whether that system is a school system, a family unit, or an organization where one works, it requires effort on the part of each person to ensure that goals are met.

Therefore, adults are charged with consciously setting examples for children with regard to relationship building, morals, and values. These are all a part of the learning process, and lessons and tests are provided to that end. For example, schools try to provide some anti-bullying and diversity training in bits and pieces that speak to morals and values, but these just scratch the surface.

A holistic approach like systems thinking may provide a better solution. For example, the underlying problem with bullying is that some children do not recognize their connectedness to others. As it relates to studies, there is also a "disconnect" in studying different subject areas in school. All of the subject areas can be tied to one another effortlessly if parents and teachers took a systemic approach to teaching and learning and helped children to find the connections in the subject areas that they study each day.

## SYSTEMS THINKING: ENDLESS LESSONS FOR CHILDREN

We often take the delicate nature of all the systems we encounter on a daily basis for granted; rarely do many of us stop to think about how important every part is to the whole. Try driving a car after a water hose has been disconnected or after the brake fluid has escaped. These things will prove to be important in the function of a car.

The human system is no different. Every day each person's path is altered, for better or for worse, because of someone else's actions. How do we get children to understand this concept at an early age?

There are so many lessons in education that fall under the umbrella of systems thinking. Basically, systems thinking revolves around the connectivity of things. These elements can be identified in just about any lesson. For example, geography provides a great opportunity to discuss systems thinking with children.

When children explore the continents and study how the continents were all once connected at one time during the late Paleozoic period, this allows students to view the now-separate continents as parts of a whole, and children can study different lands and people from that perspective—the perspective that we are all intrinsically connected.

In addition, there are so many scientific links that can be made. Remember chemistry class? Just looking at the chemical elements of the periodic table of elements chart, and seeing how the elements come together to form a variety of compounds, gives us an idea of how all matter is connected.

For instance, in the compound $H^2O$ (water), hydrogen is not more important than oxygen, as both are equally necessary to create water. Other examples of important links are the links between the environment and human illnesses, or how one part of the body, if diseased, can impact the whole human body.

When children view themselves as part of a system, they begin to recognize systems all around them. They can become aware of patterns everywhere, and they have a better understanding of how systems thinking can be applied to their lives.

## ACTIVITIES FOR INTRODUCING SYSTEMS THINKING TO CHILDREN AT HOME OR AT SCHOOL

1. Help students make simple systemic connections that are seamless and easy to understand, such as reviewing family ancestry and looking at their family as a system, guiding children to understand that one person preceded the next and that each person born into the family was important to those born down the line. Children don't assume these connections. Ask questions such as, What did each person have to do to ensure the survival of the next generation? In other words, talk about the process and the forethought of each ancestor, foster parent, or adoptive parent.

2. Another great lesson around systems could focus on subject areas that children study throughout their elementary, middle grades, and high school years. For example, allow students the opportunity to write or verbalize how the subject areas and skills that they study in school are all connected, such as mathematics and science, reading and writing—which occur in all classes at some point—and technology, which is used in all classrooms and can be applied to any of the subject areas. These are concrete examples to which children can easily relate, and they shows how one thing that seems to be isolated can be intertwined with other parts.

3. Children can study the impact that systems have on one another. For example, when one system is strong, it then supports other systems. However, when a system is weak, that system, if plagued with problems, can result in the weakening of other systems.

4. Ask children to name a system, or give them an example of a system. Once the system has been identified, ask children to name all other systems that are affected by that system. For example, the banking system. . . . What other systems does it affect?

5. Ask children to create a system for accomplishing a task. It could be something as simple as completing household chores. Ask them whom they rely on to accomplish their chores. For example, will they need a

family member to supply the cleaning products? What does that entail? One of the replies might be that their parents would have to work in order to earn the money to supply the products. So, the student realizes that even accomplishing something as mundane as household chores depends on other systems. A parent or teacher can take this lesson a step further and ask, What if the store does not have the necessary products in stock? Yet again, another system comes into play that can help or prevent chores being completed.

6. Children can study the system in which they learn. A school system is intricate, and children are very much a part of it in real time. They would likely be interested in how school systems work. Students can research the different parts of a school system, provide feedback as to how to improve their own school system, and identify the roles they play in keeping the school system running smoothly. This is a lesson in systemic thinking that children can easily apply to their own lives since they spend much of their time in schools.

If children are to learn how systems succeed, they must first understand why systems fail. Both at home and in schools, children can study systems. The systems they study could include hospitals that deliver poor care to patients, schools where a high percentage of children repeatedly do not meet educational goals, prison systems with high levels of violence and recidivism rates, and companies that apply for bankruptcy or were forced to close their doors and let go of employees.

Creative and critical thinking comes into play when students can figure out how to keep a system afloat and thriving, as well as how they fail. That concept can apply to their school system, family unit, or even the system in which they work (depending on the age of the student and whether or not the student is employed). There are lessons around systems thinking that are relevant to all grade levels. Every student can learn about systems and apply systems thinking to real life at every juncture of their development.

When most people think of systems, they think of rigid, confined thinking. But systems thinking is not as limiting as some might imagine. The lessons associated with systems thinking free the learner to make endless connections that they might not otherwise have the insight to make. It forces children to look beyond the information that is presented to them.

The study of systems leads the learner to investigate, seek cause and effect, and try to understand how specific events impact various other systems. So, students don't just absorb information; they dissect it and under-stand its connection to the world. Through systems thinking, children are always seeking to make links between systems.

Every strong system had a plan—a design that was intentional and meant to last. Another great lesson around systems thinking is that a child will learn to plan long term. Shortsighted plans are not typically born from those who study systems. Usually, short-term goals are generated by people who are shortsighted and typically do not approach problems from a systemic per-spective. Children who study systems thinking learn to create systems (ways of constructing or problem-solving) and develop goals that consider their impact on other systems.

These children will keep the long-term goals in mind as they think about the impact of their design (whatever that design may be) on other people, organizations, and environments. The systems they may consider impacting could include: ecological, social, enterprise, service, and legal. The list of various types of systems is endless.

Children learn that every smaller system is a part of a larger one. From that perspective, everything is connected, and there is a balance that must be respected. Because one system feeds into another, teachers of systems think-ing (whether it is an actual teacher or a parent) should provide children with visual examples of the effect of systems.

Also, many children are visual learners, and most will learn and remem-ber what they've learned by having hands-on experiences. Encouraging chil-dren to create different types of systems, and giving them systemic problems to solve (from which there are many to choose), help children to better understand how systems work.

For example, children can be asked to find solutions to problems, from issues plaguing the ecosystem to factory safety issues. They will first need to understand all parts of a particular system before they can offer solutions to a problem.

## USING SYSTEMS THINKING TO PROBLEM-SOLVE

1. Outline every major part of the system.
2. Identify the problem(s).
3. If there is more than one problem, identify which problems overlap, and how problems fuel one another.
4. Identify other systems that support this system.

5. List other systems that this system impacts (both negatively and positively).
6. List any current obstacles to overcoming the problem.
7. Identify strengths in the system.
8. Brainstorm how the strengths in the system could be used to correct the issues.
9. Brainstorm solutions—considering human resources, material resources, and possible changes to the system that might solve the problem.
10. Create a step-by-step outline of how the problem could be solved. More than one solution is welcome.

There are myriad ways to solve most problems. Active, continual problem-solving is a way to quickly move children out of the gray zone in education. Applying systems thinking to problem-solving keeps children's minds engaged.

This method of learning provides children with more opportunities to demonstrate their strengths. On the contrary, teaching to the test prepares children to remember information that seems important for test taking. Although testing is necessary and has its place in education, there is a greater need for children to learn more about the world around them—political systems, other social systems, and how and why things are engineered in a particular way.

Society needs more innovators. They will need to be developed in our schools. Parents can support these efforts at home, as well, and they should. In recent years, there has been more censorship of classic books in schools, more emphasis on political correctness, and a primary focus on testing. It is time to strike a balance in how we educate our future generations. Helping children make logical connections is a step in the right direction.

## SUMMARY: BENEFITS FOR CHILDREN WHO STUDY SYSTEMS

- Much of learning is about making good associations—connecting one concept to another. Teaching children about systems helps children to do just that. When studying systems, children are engaged in making connections between different types of systems.
- When children are asked to think critically, they are often asked to predict the outcome. When studying systems, a child is always looking for how

one change in a system will influence or change another system. This creates good exercises in critical thinking. Children are forced to think of multiple scenarios and multiple outcomes.

- Wherein testing can limit children's responses, studying systems is infinite by nature. There are numerous scenarios and outcomes that can occur by adding or detracting from a system. Therefore, systems thinking becomes a gateway to open-minded discussions and immeasurable possibilities.
- When studying systems, there is no room for scripted lessons, and so there are no definitive answers. Children examine the information given to them, draw on their background experiences, and cross-reference information in order to predict how one system might impact another. In the computer age, these three qualities, which help children develop as good learners, can get lost. By teaching children to analyze systems, children continually employ these skills.
- By studying life through a systemic lens, children can develop an intelligent worldview. They will notice patterns where others may not, think about all possibilities before making decisions, reflect on the impact their actions may have on a system, and will likely be good team players in the truest sense.

There are multiple disadvantages for children who land in a gray zone in education. They run the risk of being herded, in a sense, and not just by the media, merchants, and politicians, but also by educators. Children who are cultivated by test-driven school systems are in danger of being poorly educated in universities, because they will not be accustomed to making vast connections and questioning information that is presented to them.

Miyazaki (2013) said it best in the film *The Wind Rises*: "But remember this, Japanese boy . . . airplanes are not tools for war. They are not for making money. Airplanes are beautiful dreams. Engineers turn dreams into reality." What Mayazaki expresses here is that a person can be knowledgeable about a topic, but applying theory to bring a thought into tangible existence is yet another deeper layer to learning. This type of thinking cannot be developed simply by preparing children to take tests, which is the current thinking in most public schools.

Having the ability to bring ideas to fruition is different from simply learning facts in school. Those who can engineer are people who set themselves apart from others. They not only possess knowledge, but they apply it in very creative ways. Shouldn't education aim to produce young adults who have the capability to create—to be pioneers?

What sets engineers apart from others? They can take an idea and create something useful, well-planned, and efficient. If all children possessed the simple knowledge of how to fully follow through on their ideas—being able to create something tangible from their thoughts—this would provide great self-satisfaction and could lead children to want to further explore and create. Like engineers, children would first need to understand basic systems and how they work.

There are so many ways to approach learning, but the key is for parents and educators to determine how to get the most leverage out of the time that kids spend learning different skills. One intelligent approach is to help children see the endless connections there are in the world.

Systems thinking is a way to approach learning that encourages learners to keep questioning long after a lesson has ended. Systems thinking leads a child to make a series of connections. Because there are so many systems in the world—and even beyond—the lessons will be lifelong. Undoubtedly, this methodology can be applied throughout a child's life, and it will keep him/her in a consistent state of critical thought.

*Chapter Eight*

# Immigration: An Unspoken Gray Area in Education

I have opinions of my own, strong opinions, but I don't always agree with them. —George H. W. Bush

## IMMIGRATION: HOW ARE WE DOING?

When the topic of systems thinking arises, there is not a more intricate system to be found than that of a school system. When we look closely at the population of students found in today's schools, there are direct links between various student populations and the reasons schools succeed and why they sometimes struggle. One growing population in schools in many countries is immigrant children. Some enter countries legally, while others do not. So, how does immigration systemically impact education?

Politically, as of late, there has been a great deal of conversation around immigration. However, politicians rarely talk in-depth about the direct impact that immigration has on a country's educational system. Looking at changes in education from a systemic perspective, not all issues that distress a system get equal attention.

The Deferred Action Childhood Arrivals (DACA) program received attention in 2017 when it was slated to be phased out by President Donald Trump. Even that program did not scratch the surface of the far-reaching impacts of illegal immigration in the United States. It was a program that allowed illegal immigrants who entered the United States as minors some working privileges, and helped authorities identify some of those individuals, but there are so many layers to illegal immigration that it will take a much more systemic approach in order to address related issues in a meaningful way (U.S. Citizenship and Immigration website).

There are peripheral areas—often blind spots—that require attention and focus, but they are frequently overshadowed and marginalized by other concerns. As is the case with illegal immigration, the laws are such that in schools, there is fear of raising questions around the topic. This fear creates a dark gray area in school systems. How can a topic that impacts every facet of schooling be deemed off limits?

Peripheral areas can be those areas on which most schools do not focus because they feel they can do little to rectify them. Where is the primary focus in education? In education, such topics as curriculum, testing, and funding usually take center stage.

However, the effects of peripheral issues impact major areas in education all the time. For example, immigration, culture, and parent and community engagement all directly impact curriculum, testing, and funding, but they don't always get the consistent attention they deserve. If schools are to fix what are considered major problems in education, they must first examine and find solutions to the peripheral issues that continually take a back seat in school reform, but that also directly impact teaching and learning.

The topic of illegal immigration continues to be a political platform. It is a great topic for politicians to discuss at political rallies and just before elections, but this often falls flat once politicians take office. However, this seemingly nonessential issue is not cost-efficient for school districts.

Benjamin Franklin once said, "Watch the pennies and the dollars will take care of themselves." The same sentiment applies to school districts. When schools speak of school reform, they must widen their lenses to include those things they feel powerless to change. These are the concerns that are talked about the least at school staff and PTA meetings. But just because they are not openly discussed, this doesn't mean that they will go away. In fact, quite the opposite occurs—these issues become sleeping giants.

In looking at the progression of illegal immigration in the United States, in recent years it has shifted from parents accompanying their children across the border into the United States, to children arriving illegally in the United States in large numbers—making the journey alone without a guardian. In 2014, thousands of illegal immigrant minors appeared on U.S. soil without a parent or a guardian. Regardless of a child's immigrant status, according to U.S. federal law, all children are entitled to a free public school education.

*USA Today* (2014) reported, "Schools across the USA are bracing for as many as 50,000 immigrant children who would start school this fall, most of them unaccompanied by their families." The article stated: "It's nothing new for public schools to serve immigrant students."

However, Francisco Negron, general counsel for the National School Board Association, responded, "One of the challenges here, though, is the large number of unaccompanied minors." He went on to say, "This is a whole new wave of immigrant students that are coming without any guardians whatsoever." The 2014 article noted that, as of July 7 of that year, the state of Maryland had seen more than 2,200 unaccompanied minors arrive.

The challenge for school districts who service these children is that they are unsure of the level of education of such students, which means that a series of specific tests would have to be given. This is not a simple task given the language barriers and the varied literacy proficiency rates of these students. Also, the psychological state of these children, being detached from their homeland and parents, should be considered and addressed by school districts, as well. These factors all have costs attached to them.

## ILLEGAL IMMIGRATION AND THE IMPACT ON SCHOOLS

The strain of illegal immigration on community resources can be taxing. Many parents, particularly in the United States, have no knowledge that children of illegal immigrants can attend public schools at no cost to their own parents—but at a high cost to taxpayers. Additionally, many also may not be aware that no investigations by a school can be launched regarding illegal immigrants.

Talking about illegal immigrants is nearly considered taboo in schools today. With the small exception of specifically announcing that DACA was available to certain eligible illegal immigrants, schoolteachers and school principals are afraid to question the legal citizenship status of their student and parent populations, even if there is a strong suspicion concerning how they entered a country.

Further, teachers, school principals, and other school staff members may face lawsuits, as many have in the past, if they attempt to follow through on their suspicions. Many lawsuits have been brought against school staff and officials, even if it is widely known that a high population of illegal immigrants live in a particular area and their children attend school there. The slightest hint of inquiry by a school can be met with backlash.

In 2016, the American Civil Liberties Union (ACLU) brought a lawsuit against four New Jersey school districts and one charter school. According to the *Asbury Park Press* (2016), the lawsuit alleged that the school districts had denied access to children of illegal immigrant parents. The schools allegedly required parents to produce a driver's license or a state ID as a part of the process for enrolling a child in school. This would have prevented illegal immigrants from registering their child in a school district. The ACLU viewed this as an unconstitutional act.

Another related issue is, where might illegal immigrants reside? Of course, they can reside anywhere. However, it is easier for illegal immigrants to blend into big cities that are already filled with problems of their own. Large cities are known for their constant battles with high dropout rates, low test scores, and improving the overall quality of education. In addition to these already-existing problems, big cities are a sanctuary for illegal immigrants. These cities are some of the very places that do not need extra strain on already-faltering education systems.

Often, when a city has a high population of non-English-speaking students, additional resources are needed. Extra teachers are hired such as bilingual and English as a Second Language (ESL) teachers. This adds an extra layer of yearly costs to school district budgets.

However, all is not cut-and-dried when we ponder the question, Should countries educate children of illegal immigrants? One positive aspect in support of educating a child of illegal immigrant parents is that a country would be providing that child with an education, which could benefit that country in the long term. If educated properly, and if the child remains in that country, the child will be better equipped to make solid choices. Subsequently, when the child becomes an adult and lives and works in the society into which he has been thrust, they can become an asset to that society.

A drawback to educating an illegal immigrant child is the cost to taxpayers. According to *U.S. News* (2016), the average cost of education for a child per year in the United States is $10,763.00. If the parent of a child has not contributed to the tax system, then these education costs—both local and federal—must be absorbed by taxpayers. School funding, time, and attention that could be put toward strengthening the education of legal taxpaying residents' children, are diverted.

As economies tighten their financial belts, the conversation around immigration is top of mind. For example, U.S. President Donald Trump repeatedly expressed his dismay at the current state of illegal immigration during his campaign—continually pointing out the ills of the illegal immigration status quo in America. One of the biggest problems he pointed out was the financial burden to taxpayers in several areas—not just education. Many strongly agreed with his opinions, as evidenced in part by his winning the presidential election.

Other Western countries are considering ideas for relieving the taxpayer of the burden of paying for children of illegal parents to attend their free public school systems. For example, in 2016, French far-right leader Marine Le Pen raised the question to French voters about whether or not they should continue to pay for children of illegal immigrants to attend French public schools. This notion earned her a significant following. Is this an idea whose time has come? Although Le Pen lost the election to French President Emanuel Macron, she had planted the seeds.

While speaking at a conference to a polling group in France, Le Pen was quoted as saying, "I've got nothing against foreigners, but I say to them: If you come to our country, don't expect that you will be taken care of, treated [by the health system] and that your children will be educated for free" (*The Guardian*, 2016).

Developed countries have always thought it prudent to provide free education to children of illegal immigrant parents who reside in a given country. Now, with every bit of currency being scrutinized in school districts, it almost seems a natural question. However, a country has to first examine its feasibility.

## ILLEGAL IMMIGRATION AND MORAL QUESTIONS

There are a plethora of questions to consider when a country attempts to stop funding the education of children of illegal immigrants! Does a country stop funding the education of only those children who were not born in that country? Or does the country agree to pay for the free public education of children who are legal citizens of that country, but whose parents are not?

It would be daunting work trying to discover which children "belong" and which do not. Also, the process for determining who is an illegal immigrant would need to change, as schools cannot easily gain access to necessary information about the status of illegal immigrants under the current laws, policies, and procedures that schools are made to adhere. Prior to the explosion of unaccompanied illegal immigrant minors who have entered the United States in recent years, it was estimated that from 2009 to 2013, there were

5.1 million U.S. children under the age of eighteen living with at least one illegal immigrant parent (Migration Policy Institute, 2016).

School officials could be a huge support to law enforcement officials in helping identify illegal immigrants, as many illegal immigrants will enroll their children in public schools. Most illegal immigrants with children know that they can utilize the public school systems in many developed countries with no backlash. Do some countries unwittingly foster or even entice illegal immigrants to bring their children across borders? For example, by not actively seeking out the millions of illegal immigrants in the United States, the United States is promoting the thought of having one's child educated for free in a Western country as appealing, especially to someone who just might reside in a third-world country.

On the other hand, there are moral questions to consider: None of us can choose to whom we are born, and so, should children of illegal immigrants suffer for the crime of their parents? If developed countries ceased providing a free education to these children, what would be the outlook of their futures? For example, if children of illegal immigrants are forced to hide underground with their parents, what will be the social impact on societies that harbor these children, many of them illiterate?

Would cutting off free public education to children of illegal immigrants sharply decrease the number of illegal immigrants who make a home in developed countries where public education systems are willing to foot the bill? This is not a question any U.S. school district asks—not since the landmark Texas case *Plyer v. Doe*. This case established "law" for the education of illegal immigrant children across all of the United States.

The *Plyer v. Doe* case came about when a Mexican family residing in Texas could not produce documentation proving that they had legally entered the United States. This, therefore, blocked the child from enrolling in a Texas public school. Subsequently, a class action lawsuit was filed on behalf of the children of Mexican origin. Eventually, the Supreme Court heard the case, and with a narrow vote of 5-4, drew the conclusion that the school discriminated based on citizenship status and that Texas legislation violated the Equal Protection Clause which is part of the Fourteenth Amendment to the U.S. Constitution.

The problems that revolve around the education of children of illegal immigrants is not one that is black and white. To add to this dilemma, it is a growing problem, but one that many are apprehensive about weighing in on because parents and educators want to be "appropriate" in their response to cultural problems. If they are not sure how to respond, then the safest means of dealing with an uncomfortable topic is often to simply say nothing.

There are many dynamics to consider. In the past, the primary focus has been a systemic one. Countries have questioned the implications of having tens of thousands of illegal immigrant children in their societies who are barred from receiving a free education. Many of these children will be born to parents who earn some of the lowest wages in society, and who could not afford to send their children to private schools.

Why should this conversation be important to public schools, parents, and community members? This is a topic that few—school staff, parents, or community members—know much about in terms of laws, policies, and procedures regarding illegal immigrants. How can people address something that they know so little about? This creates another gray area in education.

Regarding schoolteachers and school assistants, they are usually simply warned not to engage parents in any conversation about immigration and legal status. Typically, conversations about the topic are taboo at most staff meetings in school districts, except when the staff is being reminded to ignore any hint of a sign that a child might be an illegal immigrant. However, this is an issue that directly impacts schools in a variety of ways. So, how can community members and parents (who pay taxes) have input in the problem-solving process if they are not fully informed and cannot engage in authentic conversations about illegal immigration? Perhaps the time has come to address this long-standing issue with an open approach.

What confounds parents in the United States is that if a student is suspected of attending a school that is outside of their assigned school district, school officials take immediate action, and the child is quickly sent back to their local community school. This can cause social tension—when U.S.-born children can be removed from schools because they don't live in the school district, but if a child is in the United States illegally, no one will or can address the issue. Residents are simply forced to pay taxes for children of illegal immigrants to attend school in any school district of their choosing, providing they live in that community.

## MIGRATION, COMMUNITIES, AND SCHOOLS

Migration and cultural diversity go hand in hand. With so much prevalent political correctness in societies, very few real conversations occur between parents and school districts about cultural diversity issues. Schools provide professional development to their staff regularly around cultural issues and everyone can find something about being culturally aware in a school's mission statement, but underneath the surface, there is a lot that goes unspoken, especially as it relates to illegal immigration.

How can schools better handle conversations around diversity and immigration, and its impact on the educational systems around the globe? When the conversation about immigration arises, educators often ask the question: Where do we go from here?

With the steady stream of immigrants—both legal and illegal—seeking citizenship in countries around the world, especially in the United States, and in European countries, there are more questions than answers these days. The number of immigrants is increasing, and the responsibility for educating their young and sustaining human life typically falls to the countries to which they migrate.

Recent media attention has focused on the alarming number of illegal immigrants entering the United States and the European Union. In January 2014, the European Union Commission released the following statement: "More than 276,000 migrants illegally entered the EU, which represents an increase of 155 percent compared to 2013." According to the PEW Research Center, there were 11.3 million illegal immigrants in the United States in 2014, accounting for nearly 3.5 percent of the nation's population.

In 2016, Eurostat, the statistical agency of the European Union, reported that a little over 1 million immigrants had arrived in Europe. The agency predicts that if current trends remain steady, that figure will reach an apex of nearly 1.5 million in 2036. This will clearly lend itself to a more diverse Europe, but how will the impacted countries ensure that schools are not overburdened and can reasonably continue to provide a quality education to all students? There is also the issue of diversity. Are countries prepared to meet the growing needs of blended cultures in schools?

Many school systems provide diversity training that deals with some of these issues, but they do not always get to the root of the problems. For example, the training that most schools have provided to teachers and other school staff over the past twenty years no longer keeps pace with current immigration and fast-growing immigration trends or the growing and real concerns of communities in the twenty-first century.

Cultural and diversity training in countries experiencing fast-track immigration changes need to approach these changing realities in realistic ways. In some instances, the religious and cultural beliefs of newcomers are not aligned with those of established citizens, but still there is a need for people to respect one another and maintain a peaceful coexistence. Depending on the community, this is often easier said than done.

There are many layers that communities and schools need to process collectively as they adapt to quickly changing cultural environments. It is easy to echo words like *diversity, cultural acceptance*, and *tolerance*, but for people who view immigrants—whether legal or illegal—as invaders, past diversity training is not enough.

Why? The training is outdated and insufficient because many of the concerns that citizens have voiced in recent years do have validity, but schools don't often acknowledge this fact. Any society that claims to not be concerned about possible criminal elements gaining access into their country, the possible influx of undetected diseases, terrorism, or those who seek to evade paying taxes and contributing their fair share to the country's financial resources, is not being truthful.

## OPEN CONVERSATIONS ABOUT CULTURE AND DIVERSITY

There are valid concerns that legal longtime residents in many countries entertain about illegal immigrants—and if they are not stated aloud, they are often contemplated in private thought. This does not mean that all of these individuals are bigots. If for no other reason, many are concerned about their country's economy and education system, and the health and welfare of future generations of citizens.

As a rule of thumb, school leaders avoid open conversations about immigration (legal or otherwise) and its impact in the classroom. However, in private, everyone is talking. The school community and those in school neighborhoods are talking about immigration issues as they relate to education and the overall soundness of a country.

Aside from their roles in schools, school principals and teachers are also very much a part of their own communities, and many are strong patriots of their respective countries. Therefore, many educators engage in real conversations about immigration and share their feelings with friends and family members about the changing dynamics of their own communities. This is important to recognize, because their thoughts often impact their work with children in ways they might not even recognize.

A glimpse into some of these feelings can be found on social media. Some of the comments regarding culture have led to the dismissal of school leaders and teachers from their jobs. Current diversity training for school staff members, as it stands, is flawed, because in many instances it only scratches the surface and addresses topical issues.

How many of those who are reading this book desire that their child or grandchild be taught by teachers who cannot tolerate a child's cultural background? Yet *tolerance* seems to be the operative word in many professional development sessions that are provided to teachers and other school staff. Are those training sessions effective?

Educators who log on to their own personal social media accounts and utilize those platforms to engage in a discourse about students of certain ethnic backgrounds should not be the most frightening. The most dangerous educators and the ones who are the most detrimental to our children are those who teach young minds each day and never openly share their deep-seated prejudices against children who have religious, cultural, and economic backgrounds that differ from their own. These educators are the real threat to the institution of education, because those underlying thoughts will ultimately surface in their interactions with children in the classroom.

One example of a teacher who openly shared his prejudices online, according to the *Toronto Star* (2015), was a high school teacher in the York Region School District in Canada. Michael Marshall was dismissed from his job after he made the following comments on the social media outlet of Twitter: "I feel sad when girls I teach decide to wear the hijab. I feel like a failure; I'm sorry, but Sharia law is incompatible with my democratic secular nation. You can have it, but keep it over there in backward land."

Another example of such behavior was evidenced by David Spondike, a teacher at a high school in Akron, Ohio, in the United States. According to *News Herald* (2014) and a snapshot of Spondike's Facebook page, he had stated on social media: "I don't have anything against anyone of any color, but niggers, stay out!!" Subsequently, Spondike was terminated from his position as a teacher.

The thought that an educator would voice opinions about their prejudices online for the world to view is shocking to families and communities, because those who entrust their children to school personnel do seek to hold them to a high standard. However, there are so many more educators in our system who will never voice the prejudices they secretly harbor, because they understand that to do so would render unwanted consequences, like being terminated from their jobs.

This is why it is necessary for school districts to provide diversity training to school teachers, school principals, and other staff that accesses the core of these school officials. That can only happen when open and collective conversations about diversity take place and school staff better understand the concerns and needs of the community in which they participate—both the immediate community and the larger one. This is a more sensible and systemic approach to supporting cultural diversity.

How well a child succeeds in learning largely depends on their mental state. The community can often be a breeding ground for how all children of various backgrounds are perceived by their peers. In addition, a child's environment weighs heavily on how a child will adjust emotionally, acclimate to a new school, and achieve academically. According to recent research, families and community members are pivotal in helping children maintain a sense of well-being and a positive outlook (Smith, Faulk, & Sizer, 2013).

Many schools worldwide have been vigilant about raising awareness around cultural diversity. School leaders have consistently provided training to staff on the topic of cultural sensitivity and diversity, but to what end? Each educator brings to the table some prejudice—that is, if the teacher or school principal is willing to be honest.

Some of those prejudices are fleeting and virtually harmless, while others expose deep-rooted issues regarding various cultural groups. So, the reflective questions for school leaders should include: Does the professional learning around cultural diversity that is offered to teachers and other school staff meet the growing needs of the community? Does the diversity training that schoolteachers and other school staff members receive make a real impact on relationship building between the school and the community? Another good question for school leaders to consider is, What supports do I need as a leader to ensure my own cultural diversity growth?

## A SMART APPROACH TO CLOSING CULTURAL GAPS IN SCHOOLS

- A smart goal to consider would be to identify those in the community who are willing to build relationships between long-standing community members and newcomers to the community who may possess different backgrounds. These individuals can help organize and lead cultural diversity meetings at the school.

- It is a good idea to bring teachers face to face with the community specifically to talk about community diversity. These meetings will be a learning experience for all involved, and will give teachers a broader scope of their students' cultural backgrounds.
- School leaders will want to keep the conversations between staff and the community positive. For example, schools might concentrate on ways the community and schools are already fostering cross-cultural positive relationships. In addition, community members and the school can compare effective approaches and then identify areas where their work in cultural diversity intersects, and use combined efforts to reap greater benefits.
- Although many newcomers to a country embrace the opportunities in that country and make a real effort to blend their own cultural values with those in their surroundings, there are some who do not make the effort. However horrible the conditions of the country from which they emigrated, still some immigrants who arrive to a new country are unwilling to make a real effort to adapt. Some immigrants fear that making concessions to their new environment may force them to relinquish their own culture and belief systems. To avoid these traps, a smart goal for a school is to make it clear to parents that acclimation is a shared responsibility. The parent has an obligation to encourage their children to make an honest effort to embrace and integrate (to some extent) to his/her new surroundings. In short, cultural diversity requires work from all who are involved in a school system.
- When bringing together staff, families, and community members to discuss cultural diversity, schools and PTA leaders must remember that for parents whose first language is not that of the country in which they currently reside, any information being shared at a meeting—both verbally and in writing—must be accessible to all who attend school meetings in a language that they can understand. Some schools will provide information in various languages, but they are not always conscious of the other side of a dialogue. There should be opportunities for a Q&A session that encourage all parents to voice concerns and ask for clarity—in their native tongue. So, it is not enough to provide the information; the school also has the burden to check for clarity to ensure that all parents understand the information.
- The school leader, along with the school cultural diversity committee, should determine which meetings will include parents and community members, and which will include school staff alone. There will be times

when meeting with staff alone will be necessary. Staff will need private opportunities to have internal heart-to-heart discussions with colleagues.

Reforms cannot take place in schools unless candid conversations take place, but this is a different approach to the chokehold of political correctness that is sweeping across the world. Schools alone cannot make the diversity leaps that need to occur for true educational equity to emerge. Most countries have their own longtime prejudices embedded into their cultural fiber, such as southern and northern cultural differences, regional differences, skin hue differences, or religious choices.

Now, in recent years, mass immigration has brought many new elements, and schools that were already dealing with their own age-old homegrown differences and inequalities in education, now face additional diversity challenges. This will require thinking about diversity training in schools and communities in a different way and setting smart goals to meet the challenges that lie ahead.

From a systemic perspective, nations would benefit from addressing the growing immigration numbers that impact educational systems in several western countries today. Problems in education will not shift in a positive direction in silence. As it stands, many school districts do not openly discuss illegal immigration and the issues surrounding it. However, illegal immigration is a continually growing issue that requires attention, and it will not lessen its impact on schools without a shift in how government, schools, and communities approach it.

*Chapter Nine*

# Taking Schools from Gray to Pink through Effective Communication

The goal of education is not to increase the amount of knowledge but to create the possibilities for a child to invent and discover, to create men who are capable of doing new things. —Jean Piaget

## THE JOURNEY

Whether the discussion surrounding education is about religion and spirituality in schools or about parent participation and leadership, it all begins with strong communication. A school is a staple in every community. The messages it sends shape the opinions the community shares about the effectiveness of local schools. If communication is systemic, it can have a meaningful impact on student outcomes and on the local and broader communities as well.

In particular, how can public schools move away from the gray zone—a place where public schools are not always viewed as beacons of hope for children? How do schools transition back "into the pink"? Being "in the pink" is a place where children can be inventive; have a clear understanding of the fundamentals of learning; and, at the same time, demonstrate creative and critical thinking. It is also a place where schools are safe from big government intrusions and state takeovers. So, what does being "in the pink" look like? First, there are certain elements that need to be in place in schools, and they all revolve around communication:

- The school is not a fortress that holds guarded secrets. As much as possible, it would behoove schools to find ways to communicate educational goals to parents and the community in a way that is both easily accessible and well articulated. For example, schools might provide a short list of four to five major goals for a school year to the community, and ensure that copies are visible in local libraries, businesses, police stations, recreation facilities, and any youth group homes and homeless shelters that may be in the area.
- No school should be afraid to discuss its weaknesses with parents and the community. Often, schools are apprehensive about sharing weaknesses with the community, because it might leave a school susceptible to negative press and a lack of parent and community votes of confidence. However, if the school and community cannot be honest about the school's shortcomings, then the community cannot lend its full support in helping shore up those local schools.
- It would be beneficial to both schools and parents if schools sought suggestions from the community as to how community members could help support specific school district goals. This is a good systemic approach to building supportive community relationships, and it ensures that decision-making remains local. When local communication breaks down, big government has an opportunity to intrude.
- Teacher-parent communication must remain constant. States looking to push their own agendas seek to do so in school districts where there is weak parent presence. Thus, it is imperative that parents and teachers in a school district develop bonding relationships that support student success. According to the U.S. Education Department, National Center for Education Statistics (2013), beginning in kindergarten, more than 90 percent of parents attended a meeting with teachers, compared to an average of 79 percent for ninth- through twelfth-grade students. Parents of younger children attend PTA meetings on a regular basis, but once children enter high school, there is a drop-off in parental involvement. This makes the parent-teacher conferences that occur at all levels of schooling, a critical point of contact for both the school and the parents. And when teachers and parents do connect, that time must be maximized.
- Lastly, but not to be minimized, is the importance of quality leadership in school districts. Good leadership—both in the leaders of parent groups and leadership at the school district level—must be well thought out, before appointing or electing someone to a leadership role. The quality of

a leader should (but does not always) take precedence over popularity, nepotism, and financial gain. Leaders in education ultimately direct the course of a country, making these key positions central for success in education. There should be high standards in place for hiring education leaders. When education leaders are knowledgeable about teaching and learning, they have the ability to also lead in the successful communication of school goals to parents and teachers, which will then lead to better communication between teachers and parents.

## DO TEACHERS AND PARENTS SPEAK THE SAME LANGUAGE?

When schools and parents seek to be systemically intelligent, then teachers acknowledge and respect a parent's role as first teacher, and that becomes a significant extension of a child's learning experiences. Whether an educator works with elementary- or high-school students, it is a wise teacher who never forgets that the original teacher is the parent, and who holds that important role in high esteem. An astute teacher can clearly communicate students' achievements, needs, and goals to parents.

## A TRUE STORY

A child's mother and grandmother—who cared for the child, Alysa, on a regular basis—called a meeting in the early part of a school year with the child's teachers. Alysa was a sixth grader, and the family wished to conduct a checkup regarding her performance, introduce themselves to the teachers, and get an idea of how Alysa was doing in school. All of Alysa's teachers attended the meeting as a team, which is usually the best method, because typically a problem or strength in one class can be a pattern in others. The meeting was clearly shaping up to be a roundtable discussion.

Unfortunately, each teacher took a turn, using words and jargon that only fellow teachers would understand. The parent who had called the meeting had thirty years of experience in education, at both the teaching and administrative levels. However, none of the teachers seated at the table had any prior knowledge that the parent was an educator. The parent and grandparent simply sat and listened, as one by one, each teacher used big vocabulary words, acronyms, and abbreviations that only a person who worked in the education field would understand. And each seemed pleased with themself as they concluded their synopsis of Alysa's performance.

Once each teacher had taken a turn sharing their review of Alysa's successes and struggles, it was the parent's turn to speak. The mother spoke, using the "language" that had been spoken by the teachers, and some of them seemed a bit surprised. She even talked to them about education trends and what they might try in order to better help Alysa in class. She then asked the teachers if they had any tips or suggestions that she and the grandmother could use to help Alysa at home. It was apparent that none of the teachers had prepared tips in advance, but some managed to ramble off a few in the spur of the moment.

At the conclusion of the meeting, the mother gave the teachers some advice. She told them, "If I were a lawyer or a cleaning woman, I would not have understood half of what you discussed here today. Luckily for me and my daughter, I have a background in education. Had I sent her grandparents here alone in my place, I believe they would have walked away more confused than before they'd arrived. Just a bit of advice: If you want to work with parents to actually resolve issues, stay away from jargon and acronyms that can only be confusing."

The grandmother, who had taken time out of her day to attend the parent-teacher conference, had just sat there, nodding and smiling, through most of the conference. She later explained to her daughter that she understood a few comments the teachers made—but not all. There are a variety of parents and caregivers in the world—some literate, some not so much, and some highly educated who may be knowledgeable in their own careers, but who will not understand education terminology.

## PARENT-TEACHER COMMUNICATION: BOTH SIDES OF THE SAME COIN

The language spoken by school district staff to parents and caregivers has to be plain and comprehensive. Otherwise, what's the point of a parent-teacher conference? The school can make the statement that it made provisions for parent-teacher conferences to take place, but if those conferences are not meaningful, and parents don't walk away with tips to improve students' learning at home, then they will be viewed as a waste of time to a busy parent. In addition, a poorly conducted parent-teacher conference can make an illiterate parent feel even more helpless with regard to how they can assist their child.

On the flip side, some parents do not come prepared to parent-teacher conferences with questions and insights. They are simply looking to be fed information about their child's progress. Other parents regularly attend parent-conferences but are clearly not focused on the matters at hand. Some may be preoccupied with their cell phones, or they just appear to want to get through a conference as quickly as possible.

Some parents look down on the teaching profession and don't view teachers as learning experts. In some cases, the parent believes they have all the answers. This can be apparent to the teacher and can set an offensive tone in motion. None of these scenarios will lead to clear communication between teacher and parent, and they most certainly will not help move a student toward excellence.

A little over twenty years ago (1995), the Washington, DC, National Committee for Citizens in Education published a report concluding that "students with parents who are involved in their school tend to have fewer behavioral problems, better academic performance, and are more likely to complete high school than students whose parents are not involved in their school." The research holds true in present-day education. Today, in school districts where there are myriad problems, consistently one can also find low parent participation.

Given this correlation, let's examine which parents typically show up for school meetings and events. The U.S. Department of Education, National Center for Education Statistics (2013) reported that parents with higher levels of education are more likely to be involved in their children's school events, meetings, and other activities. The report showed that 85 percent of students whose parents had a bachelor's degree or higher had a parent who attended a school event, compared with 48 percent for students whose parents had less than a high school education.

How do schools and parent associations (for example, PTAs) reach parents who are reluctant to engage with schools? One strategy that is tried and true is finding the right way to effectively communicate. Some of these parents may have developed pessimistic attitudes toward schools from their own past educational experiences. For this reason, some parents interact with schools as little as possible, and even more so if school staff or parent organizations use excessive jargon and complicated terms when communicating with them. So, it is extremely important that communication generated by the school is parent-friendly. When school staff and parent organizations speak to parents in a way that can be universally understood, it puts parents at ease, is a more welcoming approach, and will likely garner eager repeat visits from parents.

This will require the guidance of school principals and parent leaders. There has to first be a school-wide focus on effective communication, so that all staff and parents view it as a vital part of a school. It would behoove schools and PTA leaders to provide workshops around effective communication, so that all school staff and parents share the same picture. That running thread will, in due course, shape the school climate.

How well or poorly schools and parents communicate is synonymous with the type of school climate that exists in a community. The school culture and climate determines how parents, students, and school staff will react toward one another. The school culture is a shared responsibility between the school and the parents. How each reacts toward one another, and how each reacts to various situations that arise, directly impacts teaching and learning. School climate is identified as one of the major goals for school reform (Thapa et al., 2012).

## DEFINING PARENT-TEACHER COMMUNICATION

Most will agree that effective communication is one way to build a strong relationship. However, schools and parents need to first define *effective communication*—a term that is widely used. Effective communication essentially means to clearly deliver a message, so that there is no doubt about the meaning on the receiving end. Nevertheless, for each learning institution, there are elements of effective communication that will be specific to each school. Because every school and community has its own culture, communication needs will vary.

For example, in each individual school setting, parents need to know what teachers believe is effective communication as it relates to determining the best ways to approach certain topics, best times during the day or week to contact the teacher, and ways the teacher and parent can stay in consistent communication. Teachers need to know how they can reach parents directly and quickly, how parents can contribute to classroom and school goals, and when/if parent schedules will allow them to participate in classroom and school projects.

There are several ways that parents and school staff connect. More and more, teachers and parents prefer to communicate through e-mail. Undoubtedly, this is a quick and efficient way to get one's point across. However, when it concerns academic progress, there are elements that can get lost in cyberspace, such as eye contact, or whether a parent may have physical limitations to assisting a child at home, or a spoken accent that indicates that English may not be the parent's primary language used at home. All these cues can provide good background information as the teacher works with a child to personalize learning.

Parents can learn a great deal about their child's teachers, as well, when they opt for a face-to-face meeting. During face-to-face parent-teacher conferences, there can be a review of the child's quality of work in real time, the child's work is easily accessible, the child's physical work space can be seen and addressed by the parent, and a parent's questions can be answered without delay.

Also, face-to-face teacher conferences can often clear up doubts, as misperceptions can occur when people assume something about others. E-mail leaves a lot to the imagination. A face-to-face encounter brings with it more clarity when parents and teachers work together toward the same purpose. However, as children grow older and enter high school, parent-teacher meetings tend to occur less frequently.

## THE HIGH SCHOOL YEARS: "THE VILLAGE"

High school is a time when both parents and school staff need to work more closely to brainstorm ways to make their meeting time engaging, meaningful, and less time-consuming. Schools need to be mindful that a large percentage of parents have diligently attended PTA meetings and parent-teacher conferences from the preschool years through the middle-grade years of their child's education, and some believe that they have set their children on a solid course. By high school, many parents are under the assumption that their children are on "automatic pilot" after the foundation they have set.

Quite frankly, some parents find the PTA meetings, board meetings, and conferences mind-numbing. There is often little thought given by the school as to how parents will perceive such meetings, or the fact that many of them attend these meetings after long days of working. Most school meetings start and end the same way they did ten or even twenty years ago.

However, during the high school years, children can easily get off track as peer pressure increases. That's why it is imperative that schools find fresh ways to keep parents engaged during this time.

## SOME TIPS FOR KEEPING MEETINGS AND CONFERENCES
## FRESH AND INTERESTING

- If permissible, schools can videotape students, capturing them engaged in classwork. This can be done while the student is having one-on-one instruction with the teacher, or while the student is engaged in a group assignment with other students. Parents rarely get a glimpse into their child's classroom day. Teachers can share video clips with parents at parent conferences, and perhaps give them examples of how their child is struggling or how well their child comprehends and transfers knowledge. This adds a different dimension to the parent-teacher conference and can lead to more analytical discussions between the parent and teacher.
- If school boards want to attract parent involvement, then school board members should find opportunities to include parent ideas in the items on board meeting agendas. Parents often write to school boards and share ideas with board members. If parents attend these meetings, they would likely be interested in what other parents have to contribute to the conversation about school district policies or improvements, and it can also be an opportunity for board members to share some of the praise they receive from parents.
- Some school boards incorporate some type of student participation in their meetings, whether it's having students perform, honoring students for achievements, or allowing a member of the student government body to be a part of the board meeting. However, the meetings are far from student- and parent-centered, which is what board meetings are supposed to represent. For at least one board item, there could be a question posed to those in attendance that would engage the audience. Most board meetings are primarily conducted among the board members while the audience (who clearly has an interest, because they are present) sits through the process, smiles, and nods.
- Regarding school meetings, schools could survey parents to essentially ask: How are we doing? Parent groups could also survey schools to ask the same. These survey results should drive needed improvements on both fronts.
- Schools can make more of an effort to keep meetings engaging and put parents' needs first. For example, many board of education meetings will delay public comments until the very last item on a board meeting agenda, which can discourage parents from attending and voicing their opinions.

Parents who have concerns have to sit through one to two hours, on average, of a board meeting session before they can even be heard. As a compromise, a school district could provide alternate dates when parents have an opportunity to speak at the very beginning of board meetings.

Empathy is required on the part of both the school and parent as it concerns what it is like to walk in the other person's shoes. During the high school years, when a child's major life choices are taking shape, support from adults can be crucial, and a supportive network should be in place. Compromises often need to be made by both the school and the parent in order to ensure that communication remains open.

Collectively, a child's parents, teachers, and guidance counselors can identify patterns of behavior and work together to prevent some teen issues from taking shape. This requires that parents feel a part of all of the processes. Many high schools are large institutions, unlike the small intimate settings found in elementary or even middle schools. Not only can the transition from middle school to high school be overwhelming for students, but it can also be difficult for parents to navigate the change.

High schools can often send the wrong message to parents to back off and allow students to be young adults and take more responsibility, but the problem is that many high school students simply are not responsible. They still need guidance—and often, a lot of it.

Regardless of whether it is a high school or an elementary school, the messages that schools communicate to parents and how well schools connect with parents has much to do with school district leadership. These leaders send verbal and nonverbal messages that permeate throughout a school district and into the community. In short, educational leaders play a pivotal role in modeling what effective communication looks like.

## COMMUNITY AND SCHOOLS: FINDING INNOVATIVE WAYS TO STAY CONNECTED

How to get parents and communities to support school goals is often not cut-and-dried, and it can become a gray area for many schools. Every community has a culture. There is a way of life in every town and city that is unique to its people. If a school is to build and maintain a relationship with parents and community, it must first understand the culture in that place.

Who exactly is the community? Each school must be clear that if it seeks community support, then it begins with parents. Parents *are* the community. Often, schools will look to local businesses to support school fund-raising and other goals, but this can fall short because the school has not yet built the proper relationships with community business owners. However, most parents will have already established relationships with local businesses. Parents support local businesses and oftentimes know the owners by name.

A famous American saying—"The way to a man's heart is through his stomach"—can be applied to schools and their relationship building with community businesses and other local groups. The way to get local businesses to support your goals and initiatives is *through parents*. Parents who may be too busy to attend school meetings may be more than capable and willing to make introductions between school officials and local business owners.

Parents want to participate in schools, but the ways in which schools ask parents to participate is often too rigid and specific. That method works well for parents who say "sign me up for anything—my schedule is open." However, the reality is that there are all types of family circumstances these days, including odd work shifts, parents who live apart—perhaps one lives out of town—and many other impeding factors.

Parents, as well as teachers and school leaders, can find myriad ways for parent participation to take place. Although a face-to-face meeting is frequently the method of choice, there are other ways that parents and schools can connect. For example, it would be beneficial if family and community members could enter a code online and stream PTA meetings in real time, as opposed to having to physically attend those meetings. If a school invests in the technology, a busy parent who is on a train commute or who cannot secure a babysitter, could conceivably log on to a computer or cell phone and listen in on a PTA meeting. Additionally, a live stream would even be more meaningful if a parent could submit questions and comments during the meeting, as well.

Another approach in which parents can support a school without physically having to attend scheduled meetings, would be for parents who are adept at networking to either offer or be asked by a school official to partner the school with a business for which they work, their own business, or another local community business. These contacts can be extremely valuable to schools, as they add additional human resources for schools to tap in to.

Solving the problem of how schools and parents can move away from gray is not an easy task, but technology can support these efforts. Parents and schools can connect in ways that are not restrictive, that are meaningful, and that skillfully incorporate the use of technology, changing the way schools typically think of an involved parent. Of course, the more distant, technological options of staying connected should not totally replace face-to-face meetings, as that is always the best means of communication.

*Chapter Ten*

# Exploring Weak Links in Education

My mom was a teacher. I have the greatest respect for the profession. We need great teachers—not poor or midcore ones. —Condoleezza Rice

## IS HAVING TEACHING EXPERIENCE OVERRATED?

A teacher's educational background, experience, and knowledge communicate volumes to students and parents. Parents expect that teachers will have met certain college and university requirements in their preparation to become teachers. They also expect that teachers will be equipped to fully support their students in areas of academic weakness.

In recent years, several shortcuts and alternatives have been crafted to navigate around traditional teacher preparation programs. Some teachers are entering the education profession without having gone through the rigor of a traditional teacher preparation program at a college or university. As a result, a sense is growing among seasoned teachers that the education field has become a free-for-all for those who want to "experiment" with teaching children.

These alternative ways of preparing teachers for the classroom communicates many confusing messages to families and community members, and it begs the following questions: Are school districts gambling with children's futures? If so, which target population of children is the largest part of that gamble? Are governments and school districts gambling in such a way that they know certain children will lose?

Some veteran teachers who have spent time in the classroom developing their craft, believe that the new relaxed standards and programs impede progress in education. Some are disheartened by how easy it has become for teachers and school district leaders to earn the privilege to teach and lead children. The backdoor ways now available to certify people as teachers or appoint them as superintendents or in other positions in school districts, sends mixed messages to the public about standards of quality and professionalism in the field of education.

## WHO SCHOOLS HIRE, AND WHAT IT COMMUNICATES TO PARENTS

A program was developed decades ago that has some public schools rethinking the traditional teacher-preparation programs offered by colleges and universities over the years. Until recent years, working one's way through a rigorous teacher-preparation program at a college or university was the only way to become a teacher of children in K–12 grades. This new popular program that is now prompting a new way of thinking about teacher preparation is called Teach for America. It takes into account the many changes in the teaching profession in recent years, and it has shifted traditional teacher preparation training methods as a result, generating many questions in the process.

The well-known Teach for America program gets people teaching in the classroom much more quickly. Teach for America was founded in 1989 by Wendy Kopp. Kopp, who, at the time, had never taught in a K–12 classroom, created the nonprofit organization. According to its website, qualifications for potential teachers may include "a minimum GPA, college major, and coursework prerequisites." This is a far cry from the multitude of courses and other qualifications required of a teacher who pursues the traditional route in a college or university.

When schools talk about "effective communication," they should consider the verbal and nonverbal signals that are expressed to families and the community when shifts in teacher and educational leadership preparation occur. Each person hired by a school district who will lead students either to success or to a breakdown, makes a statement with their experience and educational background. It is important to keep the highest quality leadership at the controls, whether in the classroom, in the principal's office, or behind the superintendent's desk.

The Teach for America program is probably the most popular program of its type. It asks recent college graduates to agree to teach for two years, primarily in inner-city and rural school districts, where the quality of education is deemed to be in dire need of improvement. Because the teacher preparation for programs like this one is so limited, do teacher programs like Teach for America actually enhance the quality of education in these challenging neighborhoods. And in terms of nonverbal communication, what messages do programs like Teach for America send to parents and children of the school districts they serve?

For example, in poorer neighborhoods, where many Teach for America teachers work, does the lower threshold of qualifications make the statement that anyone can teach poor children? In a broader sense, does it say to the teaching community at large that teaching doesn't actually entail as much training as college and universities require?

The Teach for America website goes on to state: "Everyone has a right to learn. But in our country today, the education you receive depends on where you live, what your parents earn, and the color of your skin." Some of this may hold true, but are teacher programs like Teach for America really the correct answer for struggling schools? Would the average school district, where test scores are primarily high or at least consistently fall in the average range, clamor to hire teachers from a program like Teach for America?

Two on-campus Harvard University student groups, Students for Education Reform and the Student Labor Action Movement (SLAM), have publicly voiced their dissatisfaction about programs like Teach for America (TFA). In an article published in the *Harvard Crimson* (2015), they stated, "TFA has faced criticism regarding its two-year commitment for corps members and what detractors call the lack of adequate support and training it gives educators before placing them in schools." The article went on to state, "SLAM [Student Labor Action Movement] publicly demanded that Harvard sever ties to the [TFA] organization last fall."

The only answer for moving children toward excellence is to ensure that they have the most qualified people to educate them. That is a simple concept that sometimes gets lost in the quest to do something radical and different. Sometimes "radical" and "different" are just that, and they have no significant impact on an issue. In education, the cure is for schools to have good, qualified, caring teachers, and for those teachers to be led and coached by highly qualified educational leaders—with an emphasis on the term *highly qualified*.

If a law firm were consistently losing court cases, the CEO wouldn't go out and hire people with a background in medicine. And the firm certainly would not hire lawyers with fewer qualifications than the lawyers who were previously in place. No, the firm would likely want to improve its image. They would most certainly look for lawyers with stronger qualifications than the existing ones, thereby sending the message to their clients that their goal is to strengthen the organization.

In recent years, however, that is not the message that has permeated K–12 education. School districts are not always willing to invest in the public schools and make changes that will benefit students. It has become the "easy choice" to create something new. "New" gives the illusion of "better."

## ARE CHARTER SCHOOLS A WEAK LINK IN EDUCATION?

Improving education requires that school districts be in the hands of experienced, well-trained education professionals. Every year that education leaders spend focusing on the dismantling of the public school system takes time away from more "in-house," sustainable solutions for improving education. Charter schools have been presented as a quick-fix solution to public school problems, but many experienced educators can attest that it takes an understanding of teaching and learning methodologies, a staff experienced at turning around difficult situations, and a dedication to the field of education to bring about real change.

According to the *New York Times* (2016), Ana Rivera, a Detroit, Michigan, parent, enrolled her son in one of the many charter schools that have been cropping up in Detroit. She was under the false impression that her son was doing well at his new school. She stated, "He got all As and said he wanted to be an engineer. But the summer before seventh grade, he found himself in the back of a classroom at a science program at the University of Michigan, struggling to keep up with students from Detroit Public Schools, known as the worst urban district in the nation. They knew the human body was made up of many cells; he had never learned that."

For many poor and urban children, the cards are stacked against them to succeed. Without a quality education, the future is dismal, and the future is dismal for both the children and the countries they occupy, as these children undoubtedly melt into society.

Like the example of the Detroit parent, in some instances, leaders of charter schools send misleading messages to parents about the quality of education a parent and child can expect, giving them false hope. Given this, why are states not examining ways to shore up public schools, instead of creating more charter schools? Is there a conflict of interest when a government that is responsible for sustaining traditional public-school systems, clearly favors the expansion of charter schools?

The same energy and money that is being spent on dividing public school districts could be better spent on building capacity in communities. For parents and community members who have never been involved in the local schools, at no cost to taxpayers, schools can teach these individuals how they can become more involved. Schools can share strategies with parents and community members as to how to stay involved in local public schools, and how to have their voices heard. Knowing how to effectively voice an opinion and how to navigate a school system is not a skill that every parent will possess.

To borrow the research and thinking of Dunning and Kruger (1999), people don't know what they don't know. Investing time and money in building up the capacity of the people who reside in communities is wise. These individuals can ultimately act as their own support system, and this can be a long-term approach to solving problems in schools. In communities where test scores, graduation rates, and parent participation is low, some grassroots efforts are needed in effective parenting skills. Communicating with and investing in the local people in such communities, and not charter schools, will more likely lead to generational change.

While charter schools put education in the hands of all types of entrepreneurs (Strauss, 2016), public schools, for the most part, put education in the hands of local communities, thus giving the community influence. Many of the owners of charter schools have no roots in the community or any local social connections. This becomes an important factor, as parents entrust their children to school personnel. Also, having a connection to the community helps educators connect better with both students and parents.

It will take the same grassroots efforts that it took the forefathers to establish public school education, to fix the issues that schools face today. Just as with most issues, if root causes such as a lack of qualified educators, a lack of parent participation, a lack of parent knowledge as to how to support children academically, neighborhood violence, drug abuse, and mental health issues go unaddressed, then those issues tend to get worse—not better. Even something as simple as parents knowing how to effectively communicate with teachers can be a challenge. Is it appropriate for educators to address such issues with parents? Yes.

If having conversations, however awkward, about issues that affect learning will strengthen families and improve parent-school communication, then it is worth the time for school officials and parents to engage in such discussions. Dealing head-on with issues in a community is not always about coloring in the lines. Real change is messy, and it usually does not come in a one-and-done package, such as charter schools.

## CONCLUSION

Where should public schools start to facilitate real change? The most logical place to begin is to assess the real needs of parents. Public schools can begin by keeping communication fluid, and looking at issues from both the parent and student perspectives. Ask parents: What do you need to better communicate with us? Ask students: What do you need from us in order to succeed?

If the school recognizes a need that parents are not aware of, then it would be wise for the school to address these concerns. Open dialogue, and community and parent participation, has never been more important than in the present day, when millionaires and billionaires have set their sights on privatizing education. In order to keep public education intact, strong leadership is necessary. Today's leaders in education have many of us wondering how and why they rose to leadership positions in the first place. Having good educational leaders is paramount to children's success. A good leader should be able to observe a teacher's classroom and know from firsthand experience (as a former teacher) whether a classroom lesson is effective. And if need be, any educational leader should be able to guide a teacher—thus adding to a teacher's repertoire.

Most importantly, a leader in education must be respected enough by teachers and parents that the communication between the educational leader, classroom teachers, and parents remains open and is well received. Question: How respected are the leaders in education today? This will be explored in the next and final chapter of this book.

## Chapter Eleven

# Education Leaders as Chief Communicators

A leader is one who knows the way, goes the way, and shows the way. —John C. Maxwell

## WHAT DETERMINES A QUALITY HIRE?

For schools to move out of the gray zone and into the pink, communication must begin with school district leaders, parent organization leaders, and teachers who act as leaders. Leaders must set the standard for teaching and learning expectations. They determine the type of school culture that will be established and the types of behavior that will be accepted. School culture communicates a direct message to students and parents.

If a school district leader desires to have high-performing students, highly qualified teachers, and efficient school principals, then the school district leader should be highly qualified as well. However, the leaders who have the most experience in teaching and learning are not always chosen to lead school districts. Given this, is there any wonder why some school districts struggle?

In some of the worst school districts in the United States, one can find superintendents with very little experience in education. Why, then, do these individuals accept the job? There are hefty salaries attached to these positions in some cities, other perks are offered, and if one is unemployed, having been a superintendent of a school district can look good on one's résumé. Most people assume that a superintendent of schools has a solid background in the education field. However, that is not always the case.

If leaders do not exemplify what they want to see manifested in others, then leadership becomes a case of the blind leading the blind. This holds true for teachers, as well. Teachers are the leaders of future adult generations. As such, teachers have the most direct hours of contact in a school with children.

Charter schools have become a rear entrance. Those who possess an array of backgrounds can own and operate a charter school. Charter schools provide a platform for pretty much anyone with plans and thoughts about how education should play out; even though they may lack a background in the field of education, an individual can own a charter school.

For example, the Louisiana Department of Education has listed certain eligibility requirements on their website for those wishing to open a charter school. Although they require a would-be owner to include three certified teachers in the planning process, there is no mention of the owner being required to have any kind of background in the field of education (Louisiana Department of Education webpage).

## LOWERING STANDARDS FOR TODAY'S EDUCATION LEADERS

Public schools contend with the same issue. In public schools, by today's standards, the superintendent of a faltering school district can have virtually any college background or level of experience, as evidenced in recent years by the state of New Jersey and its governor, Chris Christie's school superintendent appointments during his terms in office. Some state takeovers of New Jersey school districts have occurred in recent years, as well as some questionable appointments of superintendents by the state's former governor. For example, Governor Christie appointed Paymon Rouhanifard to be the superintendent of one the worst school districts in the state in 2013.

Rouhanifard was only thirty-two years old at the time of his appointment to the superintendent position. In that year, Camden Public Schools had a graduation rate of only 53.4 percent, according to the 2013 graduation rates posted on the New Jersey Department of Education website. It was apparent that the school district was in dire need of highly seasoned, highly qualified leadership. Rouhanifard had been part of the Teach for America program—a program that has been highly criticized by educators—and he had only had a brief stint as a classroom teacher.

His biography, as detailed by the *Philadelphia Inquirer* (Terruso & Vargas, 2013), stated that he had only spent two years as a sixth-grade teacher with Teach for America, before he went on to work as an analyst for Goldman Sachs. This seemingly qualified him to be hired as the chief of staff to the deputy chancellor in the New York City Department of Education. The article stated: "Several former and Camden district employees and board members, however, criticized Rhouhanifard's scant classroom experience and his lack of experience as a school principal or superintendent." Another noteworthy quote from the article addressed the superintendent's lack of degrees in the field of education: "While a master's degree is typically a requirement to be superintendent of a school district, a state-run district requires only a bachelor's degree, Department of Education spokesman Justin Barra said." The question many have asked is, why was Rouhanifard hired to run the faltering school district in Camden, New Jersey? That question will likely never be answered to the satisfaction of parents who opposed his appointment.

Rouhanifard's starting salary was $210,000 (Vargas, 2013). When Rouhanifard was appointed by Governor Christie as the superintendent of schools in Camden, New Jersey, he held a baccalaureate degree in economics and political science, with no college or university degree in the field of education. However, it was reported that while he worked for the New York City Department of Education, he was instrumental in opening new charter schools (Drewniak, 2013).

The fact that Rouhanifard was adept at getting charter schools off the ground in New York City proved useful to Governor Christie. By 2015, one and a half years after his appointment as superintendent of Camden Public Schools, Rouhanifard did not announce an elaborate plan to turn around the already established Camden Public Schools; instead, according to *NJ Spotlight* (2015), he announced that five of Camden's worst schools would become charter schools. This would seem to be his primary solution.

How could any superintendent fully support the traditional public-school system and a mass expansion of charter schools—all at the same time? There is the appearance of a conflict of interest, especially if a school district leader has no experience in turning around a traditional public school district, but does have experience and knowledge on how to expand charter schools.

During the first three years that Rouhanifard served as the superintendent of Camden Public Schools (CPS), the graduation rate did increase slightly. However, according to *NJ Spotlight* (2016), "encouraging facts notwithstanding, average test scores at regular public schools in Camden remain at the bottom compared with other districts statewide."

The fact is, no one will ever know the strides that the students of Camden Public Schools might have made under the leadership of a seasoned superintendent—a district leader who had a college or university degree in the field of education, who was chosen by the local community, and who had actual experience in the areas of classroom instruction and educational leadership.

Even though past, more qualified superintendents of the district had not made significant strides in improving academics, this was not the time to lower the hiring criteria. Instead, the opposite should have happened: The problems in the school district should have signaled the need to raise the bar.

Governor Christie was not the only governor of the small state of New Jersey to appoint educational leaders in high positions who had little or no public school classroom experience, but he was consistent. According to the New Jersey Department of Education website, there were three former education commissioners during Governor Christie's two terms whom he appointed and who did not have teaching experience in a K–12 public school classroom: Former commissioner of education Brett Schundler was the first education commissioner to be appointed by Christie. He had never taught in a K–12 school (*NJ.com*, 2010).

Following Schundler, former commissioner of the New Jersey Department of Education Christopher Cerf was appointed to the position by Christie. According to *NJ Spotlight* (2014), Cerf possessed a few years of teaching experience at a private school, but no teaching experience in a public school setting. The article stated: "In many ways, Cerf is the prototypical education 'reformer': he never taught in a public school, never earned a degree in education, and never ran a school building. More accurately, perhaps, Cerf is the prototype of a new sort of reformer, one who leaves a groundswell of resistance in his wake."

Christopher Cerf was not only appointed commissioner of education, but he was later appointed by Governor Christie as the superintendent of the largest public school district in the state of New Jersey—Newark Public Schools. At the time of his appointment, Newark was plagued with myriad problems, and the school district needed a leader with vast knowledge of public school teaching and learning best practices. A prudent move would have been to appoint a person to run the school district who had firsthand experience regarding what public school teachers and school principals faced daily.

In 2014, Christie replaced Christopher Cerf as the New Jersey commissioner of education with David Hespe. According to NJ.com (2014), David Hespe had no K–12 teaching experience either, and no college or university degree in the field of education, when he was appointed to serve as commissioner. Prior to serving as commissioner in New Jersey, the *Philadelphia Inquirer* (2014) stated, "He also has served as assistant superintendent and interim superintendent for the Willingboro School District [New Jersey]."

Although Hespe possessed no teaching background in K–12 education and did not hold a degree in the field, Christie's office released a statement regarding his appointment as the education commissioner of the state of New Jersey: "Hespe is a recognized leader among New Jersey's education community, overseeing the development and implementation of educational programs, curricula and goals for an entire school district as well as at institutions of higher learning" (*Philadelphia Inquirer*, 2014).

Prior to the Christie administration, Lucille Davvy was appointed by the former Democratic governor of New Jersey, Jon Corzine, in 2006, to be the New Jersey commissioner of education. According to her biography, posted on the National Assessment Governing Board website and on LinkedIn, she has never taught in a K–12 public school setting. She holds a law degree and an undergraduate degree in mathematics.

Under these leaders, major shifts occurred in public school education in the state of New Jersey. For example, according to the New Jersey Department of Education website, PARCC testing (a new statewide testing system) was rolled out for the first time under the watchful eye of David Hespe. According to a New Jersey Department of Education news release, dated February 16, 2016, in referring to the renewal and expansion of charter schools in the state, he was quoted as saying, "We have a moral and ethical duty to ensure that all students have access to a high-quality school." Shouldn't the same sentiment apply to the professional qualifications of all leaders in education—including superintendents and commissioners?

According to the New Jersey Department of Education's website, these commissioners had a hand in other major changes in the state of New Jersey. For example, changes were made to the requirements for teacher preparation programs in colleges and universities under Davvy, Cerf, and Hespe, during each of their respective terms. The goal was to make teacher-preparation programs more focused and rigorous. They were "raising the bar" for college students who wanted to become teachers.

However, who was raising the bar for the education background and experience required to become the commissioner of education or a superintendent of schools in the state of New Jersey? Should not basic criteria be that leaders in public school education possess substantial teaching experience in a public school setting?

New Jersey is not alone. The state of Michigan, as well as the state of Louisiana, have made some questionable hires in education leadership roles, as well. In *The Garden Path: The Miseducation of the City*, author Andre Perry describes how the network of questionable education leadership cropping up across the United States can be traced to a few small groups, which he believes are systematically dismantling public education.

In recent years, a debate was raised in the state of Texas over whether or not to allow a superintendent of schools to hold employment in a Texas school district, if that person had no K–12 classroom experience or had never been a school principal. The Texas State Board of Education made a final decision in 2015, that superintendents must have some classroom teaching experience (Collier, 2015).

Collier's article in the *Texas Tribune* (2015) article went on to state: "One member—Republican Pat Hardy of Fort Worth—said the requirements to become a superintendent should be more strict, not less. Another—Republican Thomas Ratliff of Mount Pleasant, who is the board's vice chairman—pointed out that, unlike teachers, there is no shortage of school administrators." These were two very commonsense approaches about the experience and backgrounds that educational leaders should possess. Why are states seeking to hire educational leaders who do not have K–12 classroom experience in a public school, and/or who do not hold a college or university degree in the field of education?

Again, currently, what does the field of education communicate to the world? First, "highly qualified" needs to be clearly defined, and it should be the first criteria an applicant or appointee meets before being considered to take control of a nation's most precious commodity—its children. When there is confidence that leaders know more about education topics and methods than those they lead, then an optimistic climate is created in school districts, and parents and teachers feel more secure—not to mention, tax dollars are spent more wisely on newly hired leaders in education.

At this point in time, the climate in the K–12 education profession is not a very positive one. There are many gray areas, many of them leading back to a lack of quality leadership and a misplaced emphasis in what we focus on in teaching and learning. The signals that parents, students, and even teachers receive while navigating the education process is not always clear. So, how far up the "food chain" does this trend go?

## WHO'S ON TOP?

Donald Trump's choice for U.S. secretary of education, Betsy DeVos, who is an advocate and financial supporter of charter schools, is a top leader in U.S. education. What can U.S. schools expect regarding already-established public school systems? Many are expecting that the United States will see a rapid "dismantling" of public schools during DeVos's term, especially since she admittedly leans toward establishing more charter schools and more school choice programs.

How will DeVos's famous quote about public school education, in which she referred to public school education as a "dead end" (*Washington Post*, 2016), be perceived by parents and students? Countries that are leaning toward "privatizing" education are at a crossroads, and the road each chooses will have lasting effects on the development of not only the children but also the nations in which they grow up, as these young people will become the next workforce generation. If the "privatization" of schools is proven to be ineffective, there will be no impactful penalties for the owners of charter schools, but the damage to children will be irreversible, as they will have lost those important years.

As was stated in an earlier chapter of this book, DeVos's appointment as the U.S. secretary of education was not without controversy. *USA Today* (Toppo, 2017) stated: "Many education groups opposed DeVos' nomination, pointing out her lack of experience in classrooms or in public schools." Her work in Michigan is well documented as a strong supporter of school choice, school vouchers, and the expansion of charter schools. Regarding the widespread growth of charter schools in Michigan, the article noted: "In 2014 . . . the Free Press found that Michigan taxpayers pour nearly $1 billion a year into charter schools, but that state laws regulating charters are among the nation's weakest, with little accountability in how taxpayer dollars are spent or how well children are educated."

DeVos is only the eleventh U.S. education secretary. However, she is not the first to lack a solid background in K–12 education. The first U.S. education secretary, Shirley Hufstedler, served under former President Jimmy

Carter. Hufstedler did not possess a degree in education, and she had never taught in a K–12 classroom.

The same held true for Richard Riley, who served under former President Bill Clinton. Arne Duncan is known for steering the Race to the Top grant, which impacted many U.S. K–12 schools, but he had never taught in a K–12 classroom, either. He served under former President Barack Obama (*Education Week*, 2017).

Democrats and Republicans alike are entrusted to select the crème de la crème candidates to lead our nation's schools. Yet in recent decades, America has witnessed a wave of questionable secretary of education appointments—and the trend continues. This is a critical time in education. Educators, parents, and community members all must become actively aware and involved in the direction of public education and help steer the course. It is not conducive to the betterment of education for any citizen to sit on the sidelines. Public education belongs to everyone.

It is imperative, now more than ever, that the public communicates its needs, wants, and concerns to local school districts, local government officials, and the federal government as it relates to the shifts that are taking hold in education today. Most of all, attention must be paid to the quality of leaders who are appointed to some of the highest offices in the field, and who are paid with the taxpayers' dollars.

The recent shift in education, for government entities to appoint people in high positions in the field of education without requiring experience in doing the actual work in schools, is not totally the fault of government. Instead, in many cases, families and educators have lacked the correct focus and the willingness to stand up for quality in all facets of education. Attention must be paid.

Newspapers and other media outlets usually pick up stories about a newly appointed education official. These are typically provided to them by a government source that wishes to embellish how well taxpayer dollars are being spent on the individual selected to assume a post. However, with a modicum of investigation and a demand for transparency, community members, families, and school officials can determine for themselves how "qualified" a candidate truly is to serve in a decision-making role, especially one that will ultimately affect all students in a given school district, state, or country.

## CONCLUSION

We only need to look at leadership in education to understand where the problems originate. If individuals who drive the changes in education know little about the actual day-to-day work of classroom teachers, teacher's assistants, and school principals, what is driving their decision-making? Those who are in leadership positions in education, without classroom experience, profess to know how to fix the ills in education, yet there is little proof that these individuals have made any significant impact other than what they tout to the media.

Unfortunately, many people believe the information presented in the media, even without the supporting statistics to back up claims. Manipulating the media is how so many charter schools have been created. How can citizens gamble with their children's futures and so much in taxpayer's dollars without hard evidence that charter schools will even be effective? Small pockets of progress are insufficient proof for handing over billions of dollars to those who are not familiar with hands-on teaching and learning methodologies.

Another point to contemplate is how society allowed education, from the top down, to be squarely placed in the hands of amateurs? We gamble with the inheritance of our young. Some of you may remember when bottled water wasn't your first preference (tap water was considered pure enough to drink), when there was no pressure to purchase a cable television package (television was free), and when children could play freely in neighborhoods without the threat of being accosted.

There was a turning point for all these events—a point at which people could have been moved to action. For example, those who watch cable television contribute to the trillion-dollar advertising business that they must endure as they watch their favorite programs. Before we had to pay for cable TV, television station owners stayed afloat because advertisers covered the cost of production and generated hefty profits for TV stations. But now, consumers are still forced to endure advertisements—and they pay out of pocket to do so. Confusing? That's called a gray area.

That's where many societies have ended up today—in a gray area. Taxpayers foot the bill for free public education, believing that government will secure the most experienced educators to shape policies, but that is becoming something of the distant past. Taxpayers also believe that their contributions will enhance public schools, but that sentiment is slowly but surely disappearing. This is the turning point for education.

There is still time to flood the mailboxes of our state and federal senators with letters and petitions demanding high-quality appointments to the positions of school superintendents, commissioners of education, secretary of education, and other educational leadership roles. Those whom they appoint should, at a minimum, have some solid background in education, such as teaching in a public school for a significant number of years, and a required college or university background in the field of education.

It's incredible how parents push their children to go to school to do their best, but they don't demand the same from education leaders. Those leaders are instrumental in making changes to testing, curriculum, and even how teachers teach. Parents, teachers, and communities have the ability to change the script—from gray back to pink.

*Conclusion*

# Closing Thoughts

Schools have a responsibility for the education and well-being of children, to ensure that they grow into healthy, intelligent, optimistic adults. But in reality, schools are sidetracking students by infusing items into the curriculum that create gray areas, including LGBTQIA. On the other end of the spectrum, schools actively prohibit elements, such as religion, that could prove helpful to students in a variety of ways.

In terms of illegal immigration, and specifically its impact on education, the current status quo will not lead to a resolution. When school officials are silenced, the problems related to illegal immigration worsen with each passing day, and because it is so taboo to openly discuss in school districts, a shroud of secrecy is created that continues to push schools further into a gray zone. Therefore, no adequate discussion can take place about how to resolve the financial impact to schools, how to provide an equitable education to legal-resident students while navigating an influx of illegal-immigrant children, or how schools and other systems can work together to find solutions to illegal immigration problems.

When it comes to decision-making, where are the role models for future generations? There is a need for children to understand their roles, responsibilities, and connectedness to all of the different systems they will encounter throughout life. However, today, the direction in education is largely politically and financially driven, which is not conducive to thinking about the system at large. Those things that will be beneficial for children are not top of mind. Where are the children in this equation?

The choice to focus so much time and attention on topics that detract from core education in schools must be reevaluated. Schools' priorities should be that children gain solid reading, writing, science, mathematics, and technological skills, and that they are prepared to meet the challenges of college and careers. There are certain topics that benefit students and fit seamlessly into a curriculum, and some that do not.

At a time when school shootings by peers is a real possibility, schools try too hard not to acknowledge the spiritual side of children. And with the Internet access that children now have on their phones, there is no escape from the constant threat of terrorist attacks, and students are "educated" through the media about things that would make most parents blush. Today's generation of children needs solid anchors, like the generations had before them.

In today's society, inverted thinking is rampant. What's wrong is being offered to children as right, and what's right is being characterized as wrong. In 2017, children were confused about things that really should be simple: winning and losing, freedom of expression in the shadow of political correctness and gender identity.

ISIS is not the biggest threat to our nation these days. On the contrary, the biggest threat to our children today is a lack of spiritual recognition, an absence of freedom of expression, a lack of experienced leadership in education, and a serious deficiency in nurturing children's critical thinking skills. When children lack a moral compass, they become vulnerable to anything. The growing hole that many young people try to fill with materialism, technological devices, pop culture, and drugs is not surprising when we consider our current educational and cultural climate. One only has to take a look at the opioid explosion among our youth to know that many aspects of children's lives need to be strengthened. The hole is real, and it can be seen by how easily youth are lured into organizations like gangs on the streets or online—even groups that promote Isis or similar ideologies.

However, to add insult to injury, politicians seem to not understand that with each child who fails in school, a human deficit is created in the nation. Often, that human deficit is generational, and so it multiplies. Politicians have authority lent to them by the people to ensure that their children receive a quality education, but these leaders do not always make honorable choices. They appoint leaders at the district, state, and federal levels of education who have little to no experience in public school education, leading the public to ask: Is their intention to fix schools or to line their own pockets?

There is more money to be made when school districts are broken—more consultants to hire, more jobs created for people who profess to be able to "fix" the problem—and politicians can use the failure of a school district to sidestep normal hiring criteria. They then hire people with no experience in education, rather than the most seasoned professional educators to lead those school districts.

When schools fail, money is made available from a variety of government sources for politicians to manipulate—so why should they fix the problems? Why not simply create the illusion of attempting to fix the problems? Better yet, why not siphon money out of public schools so that they can have full control over public school funds in charter schools? To find the answers to these questions, all one has to do is follow the money.

Then there are the vulnerable, high-crime areas. According to one of the largest studies done in the last decade, a proven link exists between those who were incarcerated and the level of education of prisoners. According to available statistics, in the United States, approximately two-thirds of state prisoners had not completed high school (U.S. Department of Justice, 2009). How would placing inexperienced people in education leadership roles help decrease these statistics? The quality of education in high-crime areas should be top of mind for societies in which people ultimately cross paths with others from all walks of life.

Yet those who analyze crime in inner cities and poor neighborhoods often overlook the importance of a quality education. For example, when Heather Mac Donald (2016) discussed in her book *The War on Cops* the police officers who work in high-crime areas, she suggested that more policing and lengthier jail sentences for those who reside in high-crime areas would help bring order back to similar communities. Mac Donald also stated, "A straight line can be drawn between family breakdown and youth violence. It's a problem that no one, including the Chicago Police Department, seems to be able to solve. About 80 percent of black children in Chicago are born to single mothers. They grow up in a world where marriage is virtually unheard of and where no one expects a man to stick around and help raise a child."

I suggest that the problems that plague inner city neighborhoods, such as those on the outskirts of Chicago, could be better traced to a lack of a quality education. When people are more educated, they are less likely to land in prison, they are more likely to be involved in their children's education and lives, and they make better life choices in general.

Throughout history, a lack of education and low skill sets have led to a multitude of problems for people of different ethnic backgrounds in the United States, even as far back as the turn of the twentieth century in America. For Italian Americans entering this country with little or no skills and little formal education, the prospects for work and a higher quality of life were bleak.

Moquin et al. (1974) edited several sources when he wrote about Italian immigrants in America around the turn of the twentieth century. This quote was taken from Forum (1911): "On the whole . . . the Italian outlook in the United States is encouraging. First, of all Italian immigration is improving. The day of the organ-grinder, once the only representation of his race, has passed forever, and that of the ignorant peasant is rapidly passing. Illiteracy is diminishing, and with it the evils of which it has been the principal cause" (89).

Another such case of education playing a major role in an ethnic group rising above circumstances is that of the Irish American. Lee and Casey (2006) stated: "The Irish immigrants of the mid-nineteenth century were certainly the poorest and most disadvantaged the United States had seen. While prejudice has a way of producing its own statistics, the Irish of the famine era topped the charts in figures for arrest, imprisonment, and confinement in poorhouses and mental hospitals in both the United States and Britain" (367). This was how the Irish were perceived in the mid-nineteenth century, but fast-forward sixty years later, to see how education played a significant role in improving the Irish American's image and career prospects.

"As wives and mothers, Irish women dominated the Irish home in America, as they had in rural Ireland. They handled family financial matters and were ambitious for their children. Because they retained the traditional Irish value for education, Irish women fostered the group occupational and social mobility of the Irish—they were key to the movement of the Irish into the American middle-class. . . . Few daughters of Irish domestics followed their mothers into service. . . . Janet Nolan asserts that by 1900–1910, Irish American females became "one of the largest groups among public school elementary teachers, constituting one quarter of the teachers in Providence and Boston and fully a third of the teachers in New York and Chicago" (346).

It's an age-old story that has the same ending: When the quality of education improves, so does everything else. The same remains true today.

# Selected Bibliography

Administration of Jimmy Carter (September 23, 1978). "Aliquippa, Pennsylvania, Remarks and a Question-and-Answer Session at a Town Meeting—President Jimmy Carter." Retrieved June 6, 2015. From http://www.presidency.ucsb.edu/jimmy_carter.php.

Agence France-Presse in Paris (December 8, 2016). "Marine Le Pen: No free education for children of 'illegal immigrants.'" *The Guardian*, Paris. Retrieved September 18, 2017. From https://www.theguardian.com/world/2016/dec/08/marine-le-pen-says-no-free-education-for-children-of-illegal-immigrants.

Alexander, B. (March 4, 2017). "Backlash Grows Over Disney's Gay 'Beauty and the Beast' Character." *USA Today*. Retrieved September 18, 2017. From https://www.usatoday.com/story/life/movies/2017/03/04/russia-beauty-and-beast-ban-due-over-gay-character-lefoux/98743116/.

Allen, W. H. (December 1958). "What's Wrong with New York Schools?" *The American Mercury*, December 1958, pp. 36–42. Retrieved September 18, 2017. From *UNZ.org*, http://www.unz.com/print/AmMercury-1958dec-00036/.

American Federation of Teachers (n.d.). "History." Retrieved September 16, 2017. From https://www.aft.org/about/history.

Boghani, P. (June 30, 2015). "When Transgender Kids Transition, Medical Risks Are Both Known and Unknown." PBS, *FrontLine*. Retrieved September 18, 2017. From http://www.pbs.org/wgbh/frontline/article/when-transgender-kids-transition-medical-risks-are-both-known-and-unknown/.

Buckley, W. F. Jr. (1966). "Position Paper: Whatever Became of Education?" In *The Unmaking of a Mayor*. New York: Viking.

Capps, R., M. Fix, & J. Zong (January, 2016). "A Profile of U.S. Children with Unauthorized Immigrant Parents." Retrieved September 18, 2017. From https://www.migrationpolicy.org/research/profile-us-children-unauthorized-immigrant-parents.

Carpenter, J. (March, 2015). "Shuttered: Florida's Failed Charter Schools: A Four-Part Series." *NaplesNews.com*. From http://archive.naplesnews.com/news/education/shuttered-floridas-failed-charter-schools-ep-595749103-336389581.html/.

Celis III, W. (January 5, 1993). "Schools Across U.S. Cautiously Adding Lessons on Gay Life." Retrieved June 6, 2015. From http://www.nytimes.com/1993/01/06/us/schools-across-us-cautiously-adding-lessons-on-gay-life.html?pagewanted=all&mcubz=3.

Centers for Disease Control and Prevention (2016). "Understanding School Violence: Fact Sheet 2016." Retrieved September 18, 2017. From https://www.cdc.gov/violenceprevention/pdf/school_violence_fact_sheet-a.pdf.

Chalvire, P. (December 7, 2015). "Santa Rosa Students Protest, Say District Reprimanded Teacher For Talking about God." KGBT, *4ValleyCentral.com*. Retrieved September 18, 2017. From http://valleycentral.com/news/local/santa-rosa-students-protest-say-district-un fairly-punished-teacher-for-talking-about-god.

Clark, A. (2015). "Cerf Narrowly Wins Approval to Become Newark Schools' Chief." New Jersey Advance Media for *NJ.com*. Retrieved September 18, 2017. From http://www .nj.com/education/2015/07/state_board_approves_cerf_as_newark_superintendent.html.

Cohn, D. & A. Caumont (March 31, 2016). "10 Demographic Trends that Are Shaping the U.S. and the World." *PewResearch.org*. Retrieved September 16, 2017. From http://www.pewresearch.org/fact-tank/2016/03/31/10-demographic-trends-that-are-shaping-the-u-s-and-the-world/.

Collier, K. (August 16, 2016). "Failing Texas Schools Facing Tougher State Intervention." *Texas Tribune*. Retrieved September 18, 2017. From https://www.texastribune.org/2016/08/16/failing-schools-facing-tougher-state-intervention/.

Collier, K. (November 8, 2015). "SBOE: School Boards Can't Hire Just Anyone as Superintendent." *Texas Tribune*. Retrieved September 18, 2017. From https://www.texastribune.org/2015/11/18/sboe-school-boards-cant-hire-any-old-superintenden/.

Covey, S. R. (1989). *The 7 Habits of Highly Effective People: Powerful Lessons in Personal Change*. New York: Simon & Schuster.

Crotty, J. M. (2012). "Global Private Tutoring Market Will Surpass $102.8 Billion by 2018." *Forbes.com*. Retrieved June 6, 2015. From https://www.forbes.com/sites/jamesmarshall-crotty/2012/10/30/global-private-tutoring-market-will-surpass-102-billion-by-2018/.

Davis, J. H. & M. Apuzzo (May 12, 2016). "U.S. Directs Public Schools to Allow Transgender Access to Restrooms." *New York Times*. Retrieved September 18, 2017. From https://www.nytimes.com/2016/05/13/us/politics/obama-administration-to-issue-decree-on-trans gender-access-to-school-restrooms.html?mcubz=1.

Davis, L. S. (April 18, 2017). "My Daughter Is Not Transgender. She's a Tomboy. *New York Times*. Retrieved September 18, 2017. From https://www.nytimes.com/2017/04/18/opinion/my-daughter-is-not-transgender-shes-a-tomboy.html.

Department of Education, State of New Jersey (2013). "2013 Graduation Rates." Retrieved September 18, 2017. From http://www.state.nj.us/education/data/grate/2013/.

DeRuy, E. (2017). "What Makes Betsy DeVos Such an Unusual Nominee for Education Secretary." *The Atlantic*. Retrieved September 18, 2017. From https://www.theatlantic.com/education/archive/2017/01/what-makes-betsy-devos-such-an-unusual-nominee-for-education-secretary/513581/.

Dillon, S. (October 9, 2009). "Study Finds High Rate of Imprisonment among Dropouts." *New York Times*. Retrieved September 18, 2017. From http://www.nytimes.com/2009/10/09/edu cation/09dropout.html.

Drewniak, M., ed. (August 21, 2013). "Governor Christie Names Paymon Rouhanifard Superintendent of Camden Public Schools." Retrieved August 14, 2017. From http://nj.gov/governor/news/news/552013/approved/20130821b.html.

Easton, D. (1965). *A Systems Analysis of Political Life*. New York: Wiley.

The Editors of Encyclopædia Britannica (Last updated April 2018). "Scopes Trial." From https://www.britannica.com/event/Scopes-Trial.

Eilperin, J. & E. Brown (May 5, 2016). "Obama Administration Directs Schools to Accomodate Transgender Students." *Washington Post*. Retrieved September 18, 2017. From https://

www.washingtonpost.com/politics/obama-administration-to-instruct-schools-to-accommo date-transgender-students/2016/05/12/0ed1c50e-18ab-11e6-aa55-670cabef46e0_story.html.

Freedom Forum Institute (n.d.). First Amendment Center, Vanderbilt University, and The Newseum. Retrieved June 6, 2015. From http://www.firstamendmentcenter.org/.

Garcia, B. (2011). "Students Punished for Saying 'God Bless You.'" *NY Daily News*. Retrieved September 18, 2017. From http://www.nydailynews.com/news/national/california-high-school-teacher-punishes-students-god-bless-article-1.958775.

Gordon, M., M. S. Price, & K. Peraltamgordon (2016). "Understanding HB2: North Carolina's Newest Law Solidifies State's Role in Defining Discrimination." *Charlotte Observer*. Retrieved September 16, 2017. From http://www.charlotteobserver.com/news/politics-govern ment/article68401147.html.

Goleman, D. (1997). *Emotional Intelligence: Why It Can Matter More than IQ*. New York: Bantam Books.

Hanushek, E. A. & L. Wößmann (2007). "Education Quality and Economic Growth." *World Bank.org*. Retrieved September 16, 2017. From http://siteresources.worldbank.org/EDUCA TION/Resources/278200-1099079877269/547664-1099079934475/Edu_Quality_Eco nomic_Growth.pdf.

Healy, M. (2015). "Scientists Find DNA Differences between Gay Men and Their Straight Twin Brothers." *Los Angeles Times*. Retrieved September 18, 2017. From http:// www.latimes.com/science/sciencenow/la-sci-sn-genetic-homosexuality-nature-nurture-20151007-story.html.

Hoffman, J. (May 17, 2016). "As Attention Grows, Transgender Children's Numbers Are Elusive." *New York Times*. Retrieved September 16, 2017. From https://www.nytimes.com/2016/05/18/science/transgender-children.html?mcubz=3.

Hollyfield, A. & L. Melendez (2016). "East Bay Parents Threaten to Boycott LGBTQ Accep-tance Week." *ABC7 San Francisco*. Retrieved September 18, 2017. From http:// abc7news.com/education/east-bay-parents-threaten-to-boycott-lgbtq-acceptance-week/1271930/.

Ivers, D. (October 27, 2015). "'The Diplomacy Is Over': Protesters Blast Cerf, Derail Newark Meeting." New Jersey Advance Media for *NJ.com*. Retrieved September 21, 2017. From http://www.nj.com/essex/index.ssf/2015/10/protesters_derail_newark_meeting_blast _cerf_over_c.html.

Johns Hopkins University School of Education (n.d.). *New Horizons for Learning*. From http:// education.jhu.edu/research/new-horizons-for-learning/.

Johns Hopkins University School of Education (n.d.). Home page. From http://educa tion.jhu.edu/.

Johnson, L. (2004). *The Queen of Education: Rules for Making Schools Work*. San Francisco: Jossey-Bass.

Jones, R. (August 18, 2015). "Opinion: Listen, Kids, Not Everyone Is a Winner." *CNN.com*. Retrieved September 18, 2017. From http://www.cnn.com/2015/08/18/opinions/jones-sports-trophies/index.html.

Khatiwada, I., J. McLaughlin, S. Palma, & A. Sum (October 1, 2009). "The Consequences of Dropping Out of High School: Joblessness and Jailing for High School Dropouts and the High Cost for Taxpayers." Center for Labor Market Studies at Northeastern University. Retrieved September 16, 2017. From https://www.issuelab.org/resource/the-consequences-of-dropping-out-of-high-school-joblessness-and-jailing-for-high-school-dropouts-and-the-high-cost-for-taxpayers.html.

Kruger, J. & D. Dunning (1999). "Unskilled and Unaware of It: How Difficulties in Recognizing One's Own Incompetence Lead to Inflated Self-Assessments." *Journal of Personality and Social Psychology*, 77(6), pp. 1121–34.

Lee, J. & M. R. Casey (2006). *Making the Irish American History and Heritage of the Irish in the United States*. New York: New York University Press.

Lewis, C. (February 4, 2015). "Spare a Thought For the Junior-High Students Going Through 'Exam Hell.'" "Community," *JapanTimes.co.* From https://www.japantimes.co.jp/community/2015/02/15/issues/spare-a-thought-for-the-junior-high-students-going-through-exam-hell/#.WvR4en8pDcs.

Louisiana Department of Education (n.d.). "Charter Applicant Eligibility Requirements." *LouisianaBelieves.com.* Retrieved September 16, 2017. From http://www.louisianabelieves.com/docs/default-source/school-choice/charter-applicant-eligibility-requirements.pdf?sfvrsn=10.

Lu, A. (December 18, 2010). "Christie Expected to Name Christopher Cerf Education Chief." *Philadelphia Inquirer.* From http://www.philly.com/philly/news/local/20101218_Christie_expected_to_name_Christopher_Cerf_education_chief.html.

Mac Donald, H. (2016). *The War on Cops: How the New Attack on Law and Order Makes Everyone Less Safe*. New York: Encounter Books.

McGlone, P. (February 27, 2014). "Veteran Educator David Hespe to Become Next Commissioner." New Jersey Advance Media for *NJ.com.* Retrieved November 21, 2015. From http://www.nj.com/education/2014/02/veteran_educator_david_hespe_to_become_next_commissioner.html.

Michigan State University School of Journalism (n.d.). "The New Bullying: Anti-Bullying Facts, Strategies, Stories, and Statistics by Michigan State University Journalism Students." Retrieved September 18, 2017. From http://news.jrn.msu.edu/bullying/.

Miyazaki, Hayao. *The Wind Rises.* Directed by Hayao Miyazaki. Animated film. Yūrakuchō, Chiyoda, Tokyo: Toho Co., Ltd., 2013.

Mooney, J. (March 25, 2015). "Five of Camden District's Worst Public Schools Will Go the Charter Route." *NJSpotlight.com.* Retrieved September 18, 2017. From http://www.njspotlight.com/stories/15/03/25/five-of-camden-s-worst-public-schools-will-go-the-charter-route/.

Moquin, W., C. Van Doren, & F. A. J. Ianni (1974). *A Documentary History of the Italian Americans*. New York: Praeger Publishers, Inc.

Murray II, J. R. (March 6, 2017). "Gay Attorney to Disney: Mature 'Beauty and the Beast' Robs Kids' Innocence." *OrlandoSentinel.com.* Retrieved September 18, 2017. From http://www.orlandosentinel.com/opinion/os-ed-disney-gay-themes-not-for-kids-20170306-story.html.

National Assessment Governing Board (n.d.). "Bio—Lucille E. Davy." Retrieved September 25, 2017. From https://www.nagb.gov/governing-board/board-members.html.

The National Governors Association, the Council of Chief State School Officers, and Achieve, Inc. (2008). "Benchmarking for Success: Ensuring U.S. Students Receive a World-Class Education." Retrieved September 18, 2017. From https://www.achieve.org/publications/benchmarking-success-ensuring-us-students-receive-world-class-education.

Nayak, S. (January 5, 2016). "'The Best Education System in the World' Putting Stress on Singaporean Children." *ABC.net.* Retrieved November 21, 2015. From http://www.abc.net.au/news/2016-01-06/best-education-system-putting-stress-on-singaporean-children/6831964.

Nikolas, A. (2014). "It's Not Just *Frozen*: Most Disney Movies Are Pro-Gay." *The Atlantic.* Retrieved September 18, 2017. From https://www.theatlantic.com/entertainment/archive/2014/04/its-not-just-frozen-disney-has-always-been-subtly-pro-gay/361060/.

Perry, A. M. (2011). *The Garden Path: The Miseducation of a City*. New Orleans: UNO Press.

Postman, N. (1996). *End of Education: Redefining the Value of School*. New York: Vintage.

Ravitch, D. (November 25, 2013). "Why So Many Parents Hate Common Core." *CNN.com*. https://www.cnn.com/2013/11/25/opinion/ravitch-common-core-standards/index.html.

Rice, C. (2017). *Democracy: Stories from the Long Road to Freedom*. New York: Twelve.

Rich, M. (June 30, 2014). "Math Under Common Core Has Even Parents Stumbling." *New York Times*. Retrieved September 18, 2017. From https://www.nytimes.com/2014/06/30/us/math-under-common-core-has-even-parents-stumbling.html.

Richardson, B. (August 24, 2016). "Born Gay or Transgender: Little Evidence to Support Innate Trait." *Washington Times*. Retrieved September 18, 2017. From http://www.washingtontimes.com/news/2016/aug/24/born-gay-transgender-lacks-science-evidence/.

Rinde, M. (August 18, 2016). "Some Improvement Seen in Camden Schools: Blip or New Beginning?" *NJSpotlight.com*. Retrieved September 18, 2017. From http://www.njspotlight.com/stories/16/08/18/some-improvement-seen-in-camden-schools-blip-or-new-beginning/.

Rubin, R. E. (July 3, 2016). "Opinion: The Smart Way to Help Ex-Convicts, and Society." *New York Times*. Retrieved November 21, 2015. From https://www.nytimes.com/2016/06/03/opinion/how-to-make-mass-incarceration-end-for-good.html.

Sass, E. (n.d.) *American Educational History: A Hypertext Timeline*. Retrieved September 18, 2017. From http://www.eds-resources.com/educationhistorytimeline.html.

Shay, M. (January 10, 2014). "Dozens of Houston Area Schools on 'Failing' List." *ABC13.com*, Houston, TX. Retrieved September 18, 2017. From http://abc13.com/archive/9388822/.

Smith, E. P., M. Faulk, & M. A. Sizer (June 18, 2013). "Exploring the Meso-System: The Roles of Community, Family, and Peers in Adolescent Delinquency and Positive Youth Development." *Youth & Society* 48(3), pp. 318–43. doi:https://doi.org/10.1177/0044118X13491581. Retrieved September 18, 2017. From http://journals.sagepub.com/doi/abs/10.1177/0044118X13491581.

Somashekhar, S. (July 15, 2014). "Health Survey Gives Government Its First Large-Scale Data on Gay, Bisexual Population." *Washington Post.*. Retrieved November 21, 2015. From https://www.washingtonpost.com/national/health-science/health-survey-gives-government-its-first-large-scale-data-on-gay-bisexual-population/2014/07/14/2db9f4b0-092f-11e4-bbf1-cc51275e7f8f_story.html?noredirect=on.7c24857b3df3.

*South Jersey Times* (August 21, 2013). "Governor Christie Names New Superintendent of Camden School District." *NJ.com*. Retrieved September 16, 2017. From http://www.nj.com/camden/index.ssf/2013/08/gov_christie_names_new_superintendent_of_camden_school_district.html.

Spiegel, A. (May 7, 2008). "Q & A: Therapists on Gender Identity Issues in Kids." *Children's Health*, *NPR.org*. Retrieved September 18, 2017. From http://www.npr.org/templates/story/story.php?storyId=90229789.

Star-Ledger Staff (August 27, 2010). "Biography of Former Education Commissioner Bret Schundler." *NJ.com*. Retrieved September 18, 2017. From http://www.nj.com/politics/index.ssf/2010/08/biography_of_former_education.html.

Starnes, T. (May 12, 2017). "Victory! Teacher Fired For Giving Student a Bible—Gets Job Back." "Todd's American Dispatch," *FoxNews.com*. Retrieved September 18, 2017. From http://www.foxnews.com/opinion/2017/05/12/victory-teacher-fired-for-giving-student-bible-gets-job-back.html.

Strauss, V. (April 24, 2017). "Analysis: Betsy DeVos Said, 'There Isn't Really Any Common Core Anymore.' Um, Yes, There Is." *Washington Post.* Retrieved September 18, 2017. From https://www.washingtonpost.com/news/answer-sheet/wp/2017/04/24/betsy-devos-said-there-isnt-really-any-common-core-any-more-um-yes-there-is/?utm_term=.e398 234fdead.

Strauss, V. (December 6, 2016). "Why Americans Should Not Panic about International Test Results." *Washington Post.* Retrieved September 18, 2017. From https://www.washingtonpost.com/news/answer-sheet/wp/2016/12/06/why-americans-should-not-panic-about-international-test-results/.

Strauss, V. (December 22, 2016). "Why Opening a Charter School Is Like Opening Your Own Business." *Washington Post.* Retrieved September 18, 2017. From https://www.washingtonpost.com/news/answer-sheet/wp/2016/12/22/under-trump-will-the-market place-be-the-only-regulator-of-school-choice/?utm_term=.19b94cce181e.

Strauss, V. (May 2, 2015). "Are Government Officials Trying To Intimidate Parents Who Resist Testing?" *Washington Post.* Retrieved September 25, 2017. From https://www.washingtonpost.com/news/answer-sheet/wp/2015/05/02/are-government-officials-trying -to-intimidate-parents-who-resist-testing/?utm_term=.2ad4616f29af.

Strauss, V. (December 5, 2014). "Federally Funded Common Core PARCC Test Going Prime Time in Six States."*Washington Post.* Retrieved September 25, 2017. From https://www.washingtonpost.com/news/answer-sheet/wp/2014/12/05/federally-funded-common-core-parcc-test-going-prime-time-in-six-states/?noredirect=on.48f033bfbd7f.

Tennant, V. (2005). "The Powerful Impact of Stress." Johns Hopkins University School of Education, *New Horizons for Learning.* Retrieved September 25, 2017. From education.jhu.edu/PD/newhorizons/strategies/topics/Keeping%20Fit%20for%20Learning/stress .html.

Terruso, J. & C. Vargas (August 22, 2013). "Christie Names New Schools Superintendent in Camden." *Philadelphia Inquirer.*

Toppo, G. (February 7, 2017). "What You Need To Know about Betsy DeVos." *USA Today.* Retrieved September 16, 2017. From https://www.usatoday.com/story/news/2017/02/07/facts-about-education-secretary-betsy-devos/97605238/.

Turner, C. (January 17, 2017). "At DeVos's Senate Hearing, Questions of Choice, Charters, 'Other Options.'" *NPR.org.* Retrieved September 18, 2017. From http://www.npr.org/sec tions/ed/2017/01/17/510274817/watch-live-betsy-devos-secretary-of-education-confirma tion-hearing.

United States Courts (n.d.). "Access to Education—Rule of Law, United States Courts." Retrieved September 18, 2017. From http://www.uscourts.gov/educational-resources/educa tional-activities/access-education-rule-law.

United States Courts (n.d.). "Facts and Case Summary: *Engel v. Vitale.*" Retrieved January 25, 2015. From http://www.uscourts.gov/educational-resources/educational-activities/facts-and-case-summary-engel-v-vitale.

U.S. Citizenship and Immigration Services (2017). "Deferred Action for Childhood Arrivals 2017 Announcement." Retrieved September 21, 2017. From https://www.uscis.gov/daca2017.

U.S. Department of Education (n.d.). "Family and Community Engagement." Retrieved September 18, 2017. From https://www.ed.gov/parent-and-family-engagement.

U.S. Department of Education, Office of Elementary and Secondary Education, Office of Safe and Healthy Students (May 2016). "Examples of Policies and Emerging Practices for Supporting Transgender Students." Retrieved September 18, 2017. From https://www2.ed.gov/about/offices/list/oese/oshs/emergingpractices.pdf.

U.S. Department of Justice, Office of Public Affairs (May 13, 2016). "U.S. Departments of Justice and Education Release Joint Guidance to Help Schools Ensure the Civil Rights of Transgender Students." United States Department of Justice. Retrieved September 18, 2017. From https://www.justice.gov/opa/pr/us-departments-justice-and-education-release-joint-guidance-help-schools-ensure-civil-rights.

Vargas, C. (August 27, 2013). "N.J. Board Approves New Camden Schools Chief." *Philadelphia Inquirer*. Retrieved September 21, 2017. From http://www.philly.com/philly/news/local/221265241.html.

Viswanathan, B., Quora contributor (May 14, 2014). "What Are the $10 Billion Big Industries of the Future?" *Forbes.com*. Retrieved September 18, 2017. From https://www.forbes.com/sites/quora/2014/05/14/what-are-the-10-billion-big-industries-of-the-future/.

Wagner, P. & B. Rabuy (March 14, 2016). "Mass Incarceration: The Whole Pie." Prison Policy Initiative. Retrieved September 16, 2017. From https://www.prisonpolicy.org/reports/pie2016.html.

Weber, M. (April 26, 2015). "Steven Fulop Needs an Education About Charter Schools." *Jersey Jazzman*. Retrieved September 18, 2017. From http://jerseyjazzman.blogspot.com/2015/04/.

Weber, M. (2014). "Opinion: Looking Closely at the Dangerous Legacy of Commissioner Chris Cerf." *NJSpotlight.com*. Retrieved August 17, 2014. From http://www.njspotlight.com/stories/14/02/13/opinion-the-dangerous-legacy-of-commissioner-chris-cerf/.

Williams, G. M. (October 9, 2015). "To Teach a Teacher: Harvard's Alternative to Teach for America." *Harvard Crimson*. Retrieved September 18, 2017. From http://www.thecrimson.com/article/2015/10/9/harvard-teacher-fellows-TFA/.

# Index

# About the Author

**Dr. Felecia Nace** is a New Jersey resident. She is the author of the book *Massaging the Mindset: An Intelligent Approach to Systemic Change in Education*, published by Rowman & Littlefield (2015). Dr. Nace is a former language arts teacher in Montclair, New Jersey. She was also employed as an education specialist for thirteen years with the New Jersey Department of Education in Trenton, New Jersey; she worked for five years as an adjunct professor at the Mercer County Community College, English Department; and she is currently the executive director of Partners 4 Educational Change, an education-consulting firm.

Her articles have been published in *Principal* magazine; *Principal Leadership* magazine; and *ESHA* magazine—the publication of the European School Heads Association. She holds a BA in Elementary Education from New Jersey City University, Jersey City, New Jersey; an M.Ed. in Elementary Education from Regent University, Virginia Beach, Virginia; and an Ed.D. in Educational Leadership and Change from Fielding Graduate University, Santa Barbara, California.